Introduction

Historians differ in their reckoning, but for the purposes of this book the period we call 'medieval' is taken to run from 1000 AD until 1500. After a necessarily brief introduction to post-Norman Conquest subjects we try in these pages to reconstruct the appearance of the ordinary European soldiers during the last 300 years of that period, and (again briefly) that of the women who followed them to war. We look at the everyday dress of the warrior classes rather than high fashion, at the common soldier rather than the mounted knight, at armour of the less expensive kinds rather than the magnificent harness of the nobleman. It goes without saying that this vast subject deserves a much larger book than this.

Hard information is difficult to find, the more so the further back you look. Very little work has been done on everyday clothing, and on the sort of people who became soldiers. The best that we have been able to do is to put together scraps and fragments of information on which to base reconstructions. We are only too aware that a lot of guesswork is involved; but we have examined contemporary chronicles and illustrations, inventories of clothing and equipment, household and wardrobe accounts, letters, paintings, sculptures and archaeological finds.

We have gained ample evidence of the effects of outdoor life on woollen and linen cloth, vegetable dyes, hand-sewn vegetable-tanned leathers, and arms and armour, by the direct method of recreating clothing and equipment and using it in all weathers. We have consulted the staffs of many museums, experimental archaeologists, armourers, smiths and weavers, and those who practice other 'living history' crafts. The result has been growing awareness of how little trustworthy evidence remains, and of how important it is to be conscious of how much we don't know.

At the dawn of the 11th century people of all classes wore very much the same loosely cut garments that had been worn for the previous three centuries, shortened for active work, hunting and war. Sleeve length, fullness of body and skirt, and the amount of decoration varied at different times, following current ideas of beauty and elegance. But we really know very little about the dress of the Saxons and Scandinavians who had carved up and settled Europe's sea coasts, and even less about what is now the German-speaking world further inland.

Our view is distorted by the images created by folklore, literature, imaginative art, and the well-intentioned reconstructions of past historians - who laboured to show us that the distant past was crude and barbaric and that mankind had made great progress up to their own time. We *like* our ancestors to be rough and hard-drinking, living in crude huts, dressed in coarse cloth and cloaked in bearskin, their legs wrapped in furs and cross-gartered. On to this unlikely image we have pasted each new archaeological discovery; these usually indicate a more civilised or certainly a more materially sophisticated people - but we retain the basic primitive impression to fill in the gaps.

Occasional pockets of richer finds - the 'bog people' of Scandinavia and Germany, the 14th century gowns and hoods found at Herjolfsness in Greenland, and various royal burials -

A reconstruction of 9th century Viking raiders. Everything they wear is based on sound research - but without an idea of how 'typical' or otherwise were the finds on which they are based, how can we tell if most Vikings really looked like this? (Photo John Howe)

actually muddy the waters still further. We have no idea how typical they were. They are full of clues that fit uncomfortably into the general picture we have already constructed, and they provoke more questions than answers. Where we have one or two remaining helmets we must remember that many thousands more existed. Where we have traces of fabric we can analyse the weave - but we cannot know how widespread was the use of embroidery, decoration and gaudy colour.

Look at the wonderful sinuous carvings and jewellery of the Vikings - did they use similar extravagant designs on their clothes? We simply do not know - though we can guess. Mankind's love of colour, decoration and signs of tribal difference is universal and has flowered among the poorest and most 'primitive' peoples, past and present. Common sense tells us that it has always been so; but for evidence we have only a handful of illuminated manuscripts and written descriptions, fewer sculptures, and what little physical evidence the corrosive soil leaves us - all of them difficult to interpret.

We frequently build conjectural reconstructions on flimsy evidence which, by repetition, become accepted as fact. We can never be sure that a collection of buckles at the waist of a skeleton belonged to a belt being worn, every buckle still in its original position - or to a belt or belts folded up and laid on top

of the corpse and now scattered by the passing of time. We know next to nothing of contemporary burial customs, and cannot know with any certainty if the warrior was buried equipped as he was in life, or in some special way for his entombment. In the 18th century officers might be buried with their swords, but common soldiers almost never with musket and bayonet - we should not conclude that the frequency of a particular type of grave find indicates how common it was in life.

The common footsoldier of the Middle Ages remains an obscure figure. Clerks recorded what arms and armour he had and how much he cost, but almost never what he wore, carried in his pack, or thought about. Artists and writers have busied themselves with the warrior patrons who paid him. There are no diaries of an ordinary halberdier, no voices from the ranks, as there are for Wellington's Peninsular army. Nevertheless, in reading what the soldier of 1812 wrote, I believe we can get a glimpse of his distant ancestor.

The sleeping rough or being billeted on the long-suffering peasants, the hard marches, the biscuit and rotten salt pork, the breakdown of discipline after the storming of a town, the harsh punishments, the general impression of tough, enduring, occasionally very cruel men and women - these are much the same over the gulf of 500 years. So are the constant hunt for shelter and food, loot and drink; the distinctly separate lives lived by officers and men; even the wounds from blade and missile. There is some deep connection between Private Wheeler of Wellington's 51st of Foot, searching a dead Frenchman for coin or tobacco, and the hungry English archer of 1415, trudging across France in the rain, dreaming of a dry barn and silver to jingle in his purse.

There exists only one helmet that can definitely be called 'Viking'. Found at Gjermundbu and dating from the 9th century, it has goggle-like eye protection, a small nasal bar, and traces of a mail curtain or aventail. Other evidence points to the simultaneous popularity of the conical helmet which, in the form fitted with a nasal, we think of as 'Norman'. This or some similar simple helmet, and a mail or padded shirt, seem to have been the most widely worn protection during the 10th and 11th centuries, as worn by most of the warriors depicted on the Bayeux Tapestry.

Archaeology and the sagas have given us a lot of clues about the life of these early warriors, but our knowledge is too often fragmentary for us to build up a clear picture. Archaeologists tend to christen any richly dressed or bejewelled cadaver an 'aristocrat'; but perhaps such things were commonplace in that culture - or perhaps it was customary to bury the dead with extravagant finery they never enjoyed in life? We simply don't know whose grave it is. Written records might tell us that at one time a mail shirt cost the same as a horse; but we don't know how common it was to own a horse. Was a mail shirt the equivalent of a small Japanese car today - valuable, but obtainable by most - or of a Rolls Royce, available only to the truly rich (unless stolen, second-hand, or rusty and falling apart - as some mail shirts must have been?)

We know that the Vikings were vain about their appearance, loved rich clothing and dressed their hair carefully; but this is not enough to recreate the appearance of a Viking raiding crew. New information from excavations of Viking settlements in Russia shows that they influenced Slavic design, clothing, arms and armour, and were doubtless influenced in turn; but to what degree? Rich graves at Birka in Sweden, an important 10th century trading base with the East, may hold native Scandinavians or Eastern 'foreigners'. They, and debatable interpretations of very crude figures carved on 8th century picture stones in Gotland, have led some Viking re-enactors to adopt baggy trousers, *kaftan* coats and other Eastern fashions; but we have no real proof that these were worn by Vikings in Western Europe. (Photo John Howe)

EUROPA ⚔ MILITARIA
SPECIAL N°8

MEDIEVAL MILITARY COSTUME

Recreated in Colour Photographs

GERRY EMBLETON

First published in 2000 by
The Crowood Press Ltd
Ramsbury, Marlborough,
Wiltshire SN8 2HR

British Library Cataloguing-in-Publication Data
A catalogue record for this book
is available from the
British Library

ISBN 1 86126 371 6

Edited by Martin Windrow
Designed by
Frank Ainscough/Compendium
Cover design by
Tony Stocks/ Compendium
Printed and bound by
Craft Print, Singapore.

Contents

Normans: The Bayeux Tapestry Reconsidered

The Bayeux Tapestry is actually an embroidery, made some years after the Conquest to the order of Bishop Odo, half-brother of the Conqueror, for the cathedral at Bayeux, Normandy. It is our principal reference for arms and armour of the second half of the 11th century. As such, it should be considered carefully.

It has been heavily restored. It shows, in nearly 'comic strip' form, the story of Duke William's invasion of England. It is a much-studied document of a period from which few documents survive. One might say that it has been over-studied.

It shows red, green and blue horses, cabbage-like trees, startlingly constructed mythical beasts, and many armed warriors. They, their armour and weapons, ships and camps are extremely stylised and decoratively rendered. General form and construction are indicated, but without scale; and all embroidered surfaces are treated as decorative elements, the stitches used freely to add variety and decoration.

Helmets and spears are yellow, red, dark and light blue and green, as are the decorative rings and cross-hatchings used to convey the mail shirts of the combatants. Sometimes there are cross-hatched lines running at right angles to each other, sometimes saucer-sized rings. Sometimes both patterns are used on parts of the same garment. Sometimes the shaky design wobbles from rings to less certain scale-like shapes, with cross-hatching used to distinguish an arm from a body. I see no reason why the designs representing armour should be taken literally. They all seem to be attempts at suggesting so-called 'chain' mail.

On the much-disputed subject of mail, it is well worth quoting F.M.Kelly in *Apollo Magazine*, November 1931:

'And at the start let me define plainly what I mean by "mail". I hold that in the Middle Ages and, indeed, as long as armour continued … the term applied properly, nay, exclusively, to that type of defence composed of interlinked rings. Only through a late poetical licence did it come to be extended to armour in general. "Chain-mail" is a mere piece of modern pleonasm; "scalemail" and still more "plate mail", stark nonsense. As for Meyrick's proposed classification of mail - "ringed", "single", "double-chain", "mascled", "rustree", "trelliced", etc. - it may be dismissed without further ado. His categories, in so far as they were not pure invention, rested wholly on a misconception of the evidence; the passages he cites to support his theories of "ringed", "trelliced", "mascled", etc., all refer to what he calls "chain" mail; otherwise, MAIL pure and simple.' This opinion, so perfectly expressed, was endorsed by Claude Blair in his magisterial book *European Armour.*

From written accounts and other sources we know that some scale armour was probably worn in the 11th century, and no doubt various sorts of padded *gambesons* as well, the patterns of the reinforced stitches that kept the padding in place perhaps being represented by some of the cross-hatching lines rendered on the Tapestry.

Mail does not rub much as the individual rings move very freely on the surface of the body. Friction holds much of the mass in place on the rough textures of the clothing. If the mail fits well and not too loosely there are no hanging folds of rings to sway about, and uncomfortable drag is minimised. But some kind of padding was certainly necessary under the mail to cushion blows that would otherwise drive the wire rings into the flesh.

It is not clear just how much use the seafaring Vikings made of horses for their forays inland, but use them they certainly did. With the passage of time and contact with horsemen in the lands they settled, some of their descendants evolved into a powerful and aggressive cavalry. Centuries of raiding and settling intermingled the peoples of Britain and coastal Europe, and spread Scandinavian culture into Russia and the Mediterranean. The warband of Hrolf the Ganger settled in northern France; the descendants of these 'Northmen' became the Normans, continuing their expeditions of conquest by sea and land. A tough breed of greedy, quarrelsome knights, ambitious and hungry for land and power, they took service wherever rewards were promised. The knights of Duke William's 'Norman' army which invaded England in 1066 were not the united nationalistic oppressors of legend. In fact they hailed from all over Europe, drawn to the banner of William the Bastard by a craving for land and gold. (Photo VS-Books)

(Opposite) This reconstruction of an 11th century Norman cavalryman illustrates a style of defence and dress apparently common at that time across Western Europe. His long kite-shaped shield protects his left side and leg when on horseback. He has a *spangenhelm* - a conical helmet built up from four segmental plates on a frame - with a wide nasal; this is secured over the integral hood of his long mail *hauberk*. Slit front and back for riding, this is worn over a lightly padded *gambeson*. He would be armed with a long spear for use on horseback (not seen here) and a sword.

The sword has always held a certain mystique. Saxons and Vikings gave them splendid names - 'Greyflank', 'Byrnie-biter', 'Long and Sharp' - and reverently handed down the beautifully wrought blades from father to son, or placed them in a hero's grave. In crusading times the sword became the symbol of knighthood, inheriting something of the old pagan magic - made respectable by a mixture of prayer and Christian purpose. Later, with the emergence of the professional, highly-valued footsoldier, it became the common arm of the medieval fighting man. In the more cynical 15th century a French soldier might christen his sword 'Gaine-Pain' - (*gagne-pain*, 'bread-winner'). (Photo VS-Books)

(Right) Crusader, second half of the 12th century. Many surviving effigies show that at about this time a linen gown was worn over the armour. Styles varied, long or short, sometimes with sleeves, and almost always slit before and behind for riding. Why it was adopted is unclear. It was not ample enough to give complete protection from rain - but in the sun of the Holy Land some covering was necessary to stop the long mail hauberk from heating up unbearably. In direct contact with hot sunshine or icy air a mail shirt soon becomes an extremely uncomfortable burden, but even a single layer of cloth between it and the outside temperature makes a great difference. At first simply of plain linen or some colourful fabric, during the next century these surcoats came to be used as an additional surface on which to display the owner's heraldic colours and devices.

Some other adaptations to the climate of the Holy Land and hard campaigning are also visible here - soft boots, a piece of carpet as a saddle cloth, a water gourd, picket rope and cooking pot, and - just visible on his chest - a long scarf to keep off sun and dust. (Photo John Howe; figure made by Gerry Embleton / Time Machine AG)

(Left) The heavy but well-balanced double-edged broadsword of the early Norman world. Contrary to popular belief, swords were not usually worn in everyday life during the Middle Ages. Important officials might carry their sword with the waist belts wrapped around it for some ceremonial occasions, but normally the wearing of swords in civil life was officially discouraged. (Photo Gerry Embleton)

The high praises of God are in their throats,
and two-edged swords are in their hands
to bring punishment on the nations
and rebuke upon the peoples,
and to bind their kings in chains
and their nobles with links of iron.

John of Salisbury, 12th C

7

(Opposite) Plate 1:
Mail and Helmets, c1050 to 1250

(A) This is virtually the same as the equipment shown on the Bayeux Tapestry. Simple cross-hatching, which makes no attempt to follow the form of the body, probably represents mail, or is simply an artistic convention for 'armour'. There is no separate ventail here, but this may be because the drawing is very simple. (Apocalypse of St Sever, mid-11th C)

(B) The rectangular panels high on the chests may be a very impressionistic rendering of the neck closure of the shirt, or of a ventail. Not too much weight should be rested on the details of the very free renderings of the Tapestry. (Bayeux Tapestry, late 11th C)

(C) The details on this stone figure look convincing; clearly a cloth- or leather-bound mail flap hangs down on the chest, its construction closely resembling those shown on the Bayeux Tapestry. (11th C, possibly Spanish, site now unknown)

(D & E) Two examples of mail *coifs* - in this usage, the integral hood to a mail shirt - with laced-up ventails. (MS illustrations, mid-13th C)

(F) The conical helm with nasal worn by Vikings and Normans, and popular throughout 11th century Europe; the ventail is tied up by a lace threaded though the mail. It was essential for the helmet to be firmly fixed on the head or any blow would force the nasal back into the face. For the same reason the mail covering the cheeks and chin must have been padded.

(G & H) Cloth coifs - in this usage, tight-fitting caps often tied beneath the chin - are shown worn by civilian and soldier alike, for work and war, in various illustrations (including the Maciejowski Bible, c1250); and some are clearly padded.

They also helped keep long hair, when fashionable, out of the way. Fashions in hair length changed, much as they do today. In 1095 the council of Rouen passed a decree against long hair, and Henry I of England did the same - both unsuccessfully.

Legend has it that 'a young provincial soldier who had long and beautiful hair' dreamed that he was being strangled with his own locks, and cut them off; his companions followed suit, and so spread a short-lived fashion for short hair. At the end of the 12th century followers of international courtly fashion curled their hair, but only the vainest of soldiers would have had time for such affectations.

Fashions in clothing came and went among the wealthier sort for longer or shorter, tighter or looser-flowing gowns - but probably had less effect on the everyday clothing of workers and soldiers. Their garments may have faintly and tardily echoed passing fashion, but remained short enough for easy movement and long enough to protect against the elements.

(I) 'Kettle hat' or *chapel de fer* with thongs to tie under the chin, worn over a mail coif. Again, one cannot over-emphasise the fact that all helmets needed to be very firmly secured on the head to be an effective defence in hand-to-hand combat. Many sources show kettle hats of various styles, sometimes coloured as if painted.

(J) Manuscripts and sculptures, c1240-1250, show a rounded form to the top of the mail coif which is clearly shaped by a padded cap beneath. The helmet lining was probably shaped to fit snugly over it.

(K) Sculpture from the Temple Church, London, c1240-50, showing a buckled ventail; and also a circlet of metal or perhaps leather, indicating a firm foundation for the helmet.

(L, M & N) Some sculptures on the facade of Wells Cathedral, c1230-1240 show examples of the sophisticated arming caps which developed to seat 13th C 'bucket' helms securely, Note that N has a stiffly padded collar which would further prevent the bottom edge of the helm from being knocked inwards.

(O) Effigy of a Templer wearing a close-fitting arming cap completely covering cheeks and mouth. It is clearly not mail, as

(Above) The hauberk with integral hood continued to be the most common defence during the 12th and 13th centuries. The neck opening was usually closed with a *ventail* which fastened across the jaw and throat. In the second half of the 12th century mail mittens formed part of the sleeves; they were lined with a leather glove, and the hand could be pushed through a slit in the palm to leave the mitten hanging from the wrist when not needed. Mail stockings (*chausses*) were also commonly worn. The necessary padded garment worn under the mail doubtless took many forms to suit taste and comfort. We do not know when metal, leather or horn reinforcements were first incorporated into it. (Photo VS-Books)

the texture of his mail collar is carved to contrast with its smooth surfaces. Perhaps it is thick leather? (Temple Church, London, 13th C)

(P) Effigy of Geoffrey de Mandeville, Earl of Essex c1238, from the Temple Church; this effigy was severely damaged by German bombing during the Second World War. It shows, in a style that elongates the form of figure and head, a type of cap not seen elsewhere, with an attached band which encircles the face. This may be a leather arming cap to fit tightly inside a flat-topped 'great helm' and hold it securely in place.

(Q) Two headpieces marking a transition between the mail coif and the enclosed 'bucket' helm. They are coloured, and in shape

they echo figure P. May we speculate that they are of thick but still slightly flexible leather? If they are of one-piece metal construction it is hard to see how one got them on and off. (Martyrdom of St Thomas à Becket, late 12th C)

(R) The Maciejowski Bible of c1250 shows a variety of open-faced and 'bucket' helms. This one, fitting quite high on the head, would need a very secure foundation and fixing, or the slightest blow would reposition the eye slits and blind the wearer.

(S) A deeper version of about the same date shows strongly reinforced eye slits and holes for ventilation over the cheeks. The same form with a rounded crown would remain in use well into the 14th century.

A

B

C

F

E

D

G

J

H

I

K

L

P

Q

M

N

O

R

S

(Opposite) Plate 2:
Body Defences, c1250 to c1360

During the 13th century defensive armour began increasingly to include plates of horn, whalebone, leather and iron. There are frequent references to '*curie*' and '*paires de cuiraces*' (from the French *cuire*, leather), and to 'pairs of plates'. Exposed parts - knee, shin, elbow and forearm - were protected with padded defences and strapped-on plates; but body armour was usually invisible beneath the mail shirt or cloth surcoat. We have little evidence for the form of these usually hidden protections, nor a clear idea of when they first developed - only when they first appear in our sparse sources, suggested in effigies by rigid shapes under flowing surcoats or buckled straps glimpsed inside their wide armholes.

Gradually the plates grew in size to cover the entire body. The hauberk, now generally worn beneath the plates, diminished until, by the 15th century, its function was merely to fill the gaps in the now almost complete plate armour.

(**A**) A very early representation of a 'pair of plates', from a Spanish manuscript. (The Commentary on the Apocalypse, Beatus of Paris, c1250)

(**B**) This sleeping guard from a reliquary clearly shows vertical plates riveted to the inside of a long coat. Armour made of plates and fabric was not the most expensive, and both old and new materials could be combined. Footsoldiers would continue to use multi-layered defences combining plates and padding until the end of the age of armour. (Wienhausen Monastery, Germany, c1270)

(**C**) The French knight Sir Brocardus de Charpignie, c1270, wears what look like the buckles for a 'coat-of-plates' on his shoulders; and an unusual bowl-shaped helm with a shallow neck guard. Or rather, we *think* it is unusual - in fact it may have been very common, only we have no other representations of it.

(**D**) The effigy of an unidentified knight shows clearly the buckles of some kind of plate defence under his surcoat. (Pershore Abbey, Worcestershire, second half of 13th C)

(**E**) The monumental effigy of Nils Johnsson, c1315-19, shows a reinforced surcoat with visible rivet heads. His attached mail mittens are turned back over his wrists. Common soldiers wore gloves and gauntlets, which seem to have been in widespread use at all levels of society for work, warfare or fashionable display. (St Mary's Church, Sig-una, Sweden)

(**F**) This knight painted on a church wall at South Röda, Sweden, c1323, wears an unusually short reinforced surcoat or coat-of-plates, and - apparently - complete breeches of mail. At the battle of Bouvines (1214) Reginald de Boulogne is said to have been saved from a dagger-thrust under his mail shirt because his mail hose were fastened to it.

(**G & H**) Reconstruction of a coat-of-plates, based on the figure of St Maurice in Magdeburg Cathedral, late 13th C, and a drawing in *Warrior to Soldier 419-1660* by Norman & Pottinger (see further reading list, page 96).

(**I**) Coat-of-plates based on one of some 30 found at the site of the battle of Visby in Gotland (1361). Most are constructed of many small plates, but three have large vertical plates originally riveted to a cloth 'poncho' which was probably padded or multi-layered. The plates exposed here would almost certainly have been hidden beneath a fabric lining.

It must not be assumed that early armour was only worn in the ways described here. In a pre-industrial world where everything was made by hand there must have been an individuality which is difficult to imagine today.

(**Left above and below**) Reconstruction of a 'coat-of-plates', worn with a plain steel kettle hat and separate-legged hose by one of the Black Prince's artillerymen, c1350s. (Photos Gerry Embleton)

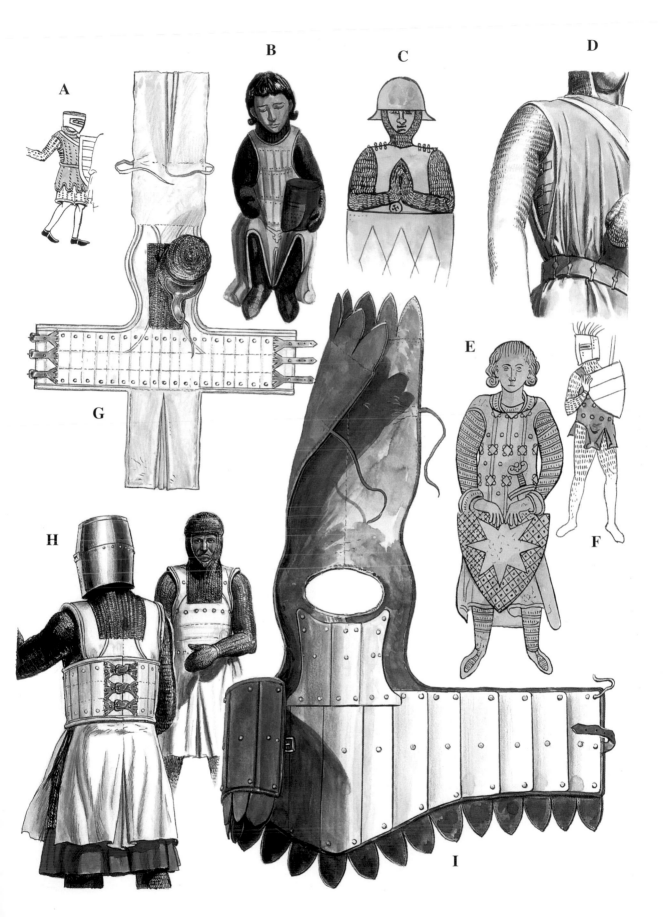

A

B

C

D

E

F

G

H

I

13th Century Soldiers

Our knowledge of the warrior's equipment is scanty, but we find a few interesting details in the 13th century *Rule of the Temple*. The Order decreed that a Templer knight - at the upper end of the scale of professional soldiers - should have in addition to his arms and armour an arming cap, dagger, large and small knives, two shirts, two *braies*, two pairs of padded *chausses*, a narrow belt, two small sacks for his nightshirt, arming coat, etc., and a leather or coarse sack for his mail *hauberk*, wide sword belts with or without buckles, and felt hats.

A sergeant, a little less well armed than a brother knight, had mailshirt, mail hose without feet (to make marching easier) and war hat. Turkish bows were included in his arsenal, as was probably other captured material. On crusade their clothing and equipment was certainly influenced by that of the enemy and adapted to the hot climate.

(Above & right) Until the early 1300s the footsoldier was usually a *villein* - drawn from the poorest agricultural tenantry, and owing military service to his feudal master. He probably came wearing the strongest and warmest clothes he possessed, with a poncho-like *huke* or a cloak and a hood, and carrying any spare clothes and personal possessions in a bag. He was supposed to bring arms of his own or those that his master could provide; if he failed to do so fines might have to be paid. If called up by a rich and generous lord he might be well equipped; if not, then hard times might lie ahead.

This man has rolled his hose down to below his knees; he works at cutting wood on a chill autumn morning, in his doublet and hood. Woven checks and stripes were simple to produce and much more common than we may imagine, being frequently mentioned in lists of livery. His purse has the very cheapest sort of metal decorations. He may be travelling with a small band of his comrades, buying food with his wages en route. We read of Catalan and Aragonese soldiers in 1302 bound from Palermo to Messina accompanied by their wives and children, with the king's silver in their purses, and a generous ration of biscuits, cheeses, salt meat, garlic and onions. (Photos Gerry Embleton)

(Below) A well padded *gambeson* or *aketon* was the common soldier's usual protection - a long tunic made of cloth stuffed with wool, cotton or rags and quilted to keep the stuffing in place. Wrap-around coats-of-plates, and perhaps padded shirts reinforced with mail and plates became increasingly common, giving a harder and smoother outline to the body of the knight as depicted; these defences may also have been worn by some humbler soldiers.

Around 1300 the daily rate of pay for the foot soldier in England, France and Florence was about the same as that for a labourer. Tenants called up to serve came armed and equipped according to the property they rented. In 1284 the Abbot of St Maur des Fossés in France called up 12 tenants who each had a mail shirt, iron cap, sword and dagger; 53 had a padded gambeson, iron cap, sword and dagger; the more prosperous among the rest had to have an iron cap, sword and dagger, and the poorest a bow, arrows and dagger. Villages might be obliged to provide a number of men armed and fit for military service, and inspection reports frequently note how poorly armed they sometimes were. (Photo John Howe)

(Right) This 13th century soldier comes from a prosperous village or serves a lord of some means; he has a new gambeson and good woollen jacket, hose and hood. His kettle hat is bright steel (though they were frequently painted). He is armed with a light spear and a knife. (Photo John Howe)

(Above) A slightly better armoured and armed member of the same contingent, wearing a woollen hood in his captain's colours. He has a mail shirt under his gambeson, and in addition to his long spear he carries a cheap but serviceable sword. We do not know how extensively common soldiers wore mail in the 13th century. Mail takes a very long time to wear out; it can easily be patched and repaired, even retailored. There must have been a vast and steadily increasing accumulation of mail in Europe, some perhaps dating back to Roman times or even earlier. With his everyday clothes this soldier wears a second pair of short hose - loose footless 'socks' - to protect his lower legs against the cold and the snagging of brushwood. (Photo Gerry Embleton)

13

14th Century Handgunner

(Below) This sturdy handgunner serves Edward the Black Prince of Wales during his French wars in the third quarter of the 14th century. Far down the ladder of liveried retainers, he has been given a long gown of unbleached wool, and a 'handgonne' of the simplest type on a pole stock.

In 1326 the council of Florence appointed two officials to oversee the manufacture of cannon and projectiles which had, no doubt, been present on the battlefield for some years before. The first illustration dates from this time - a short bottle-shaped gun with a tubular bore, shooting a metal arrow.

The first mention of the use of a man-carried firearm in England dates from 1338, when 'un handgonne' is listed among the equipment for one of Edward III's ships. Soon afterwards we have a record of six stored at the Guildhall in London. The earliest surviving example is a small bronze gun found at Loshult in Sweden, c1350-1400. For ease of handling these stumpy barrels were fixed to wooden staves. They were cast in bronze, or forged in iron, built up like a barrel with staves and hoops and, at the end of the century, made as an iron tube with a breech plug screwed in one end. The first

guns were touched off with a hot wire or a burning match, making handling by one man very tricky and not conducive to accuracy.

Over the next century the barrels got longer and the staves more sculptured, so that by the 1460s we have something that is clearly recognisable as a shoulder firearm. The earliest known drawing of an S-shaped holder for the match, also serving as a trigger, dates from 1411. During the next 50 years various forms of lock with trigger or button release were developed, allowing the guns to be held into the shoulder and sighted along the barrel.

Who the earliest handgunners were, and why they adopted such an alarmingly dangerous and seemingly inaccurate weapon, is not known. Clearly, they were soon effective enough to start replacing some of the crossbows in groups of skirmishers, and to take their place on the competition field. Despite the results of isolated modern experiments, we may underestimate their accuracy in the hands of experienced men long familiar with them. No professional soldier chooses to carry into battle a weapon which he distrusts. (Photo Gerry Embleton)

14th Century Bowmen

In armies assembled around a fighting core of mounted knights their retainers on foot and the shire levies (militia) provided a mass of infantry whose main task was to form a solid reserve to protect the baggage train - and the cavalry, when they needed to reform. Footsoldiers might swarm out to slaughter a defeated enemy; but - with some notable exceptions - it was not until the mid-14th century that well-trained infantry with pole and missile weapons began to come into their own as important tactical elements.

The increasing importance of the longbowman in English armies, and the development throughout Europe of wealthy, independent towns with a need for efficient defenders, led to an improvement in the importance, and thus the rewards of the footsoldier. The highly skilled English archer of the Hundred Years War was a yeoman, no longer a disregarded peasant. In peacetime he was probably still a farmworker, but he might equally be a craftsman or small tradesman. These well-paid men had the standing and the means to win themselves some sort of stake in their society.

Towns across the Continent trained citizen militias, some of whom paid substitutes. Some who joined the ranks were criminals: a royal pardon could be won in exchange for military service. Mercenaries of different kinds formed parts of all armies, enthusiastically recruited *en masse* by some commanders, with reluctant suspicion by others. Some proved loyal; others simply flocked to any new war, following money and plunder as individuals or in bands. Their travels and their relative success would have been reflected in their clothing and arms. Although clothing was almost international in style, mercenaries could still turn heads: in the early 1350s their Italian employers disliked the beards sported by Catalan troops, and a century later they were amused by the Germans' long hair.

In the 1340s there was an abrupt change of fashion in the courts of France; long, loose tunics and overtunics were superseded by short, tight garments. This scandalous new style spread to England, Italy and Germany. Dandies cropped their hair and wore long moustaches 'like the Spanish'. The French King Philip VI was opposed to this decadence. One can imagine that some courtiers, knights and retainers clung disapprovingly to the old styles, while others adopted the new as best they could. The extravagance of such indelicate dress and other sins were to blame - according to the French author of *La Grande Chronique de St Denis* - to their defeat at Crécy in 1345. We cannot be sure how much high fashion affected the dress of the soldier; but the 14th century chronicler Knighton wrote that 'vanity of the common people in their dress was so great that it was impossible to tell rich from poor, high from low'.

(Right) On 14 September 1346 Master John de Brunham, Clerk to Edward, The Black Prince, was ordered to buy green and white cloth to make a *courtepye* (jacket) and *chaperon* (hood) for each of the Welsh bowmen from Flynt in his master's service. Both garments were to be half green (on the right) and half white. It is impossible to positively identify the courtepye; it was probably a shortish tunic - as was the *cote*, another term freely used to describe many kinds of overgarments, including a lady's long overdress with train. (Photo Gerry Embleton)

(Opposite) A 14th century hunter in typical outdoor clothing. In time of war both his skills and his gear would translate directly to the battlefield with only minor modifications and additions. (Photo David Lazenby, Middelaldercentret)

This simple but beautifully reconstructed costume shows what can be done with good research and careful work. It was made for this book by Julie Douglass of 'Artefacts'. The references used for this archer's general appearance were the Luttrell Psalter (c1320-1340), and patterns based on the remains of medieval clothing found in Greenland and Sweden, with details drawn from many other contemporary sources.

(Below) The falchion, one of many designs of heavy-bladed short swords which saw widespread use until the end of the 15th century, is based on the Conyers falchion and various contemporary illustrations.

(Left, above & opposite) Tabby-woven, fulled white woollen cloth was dyed with Broom, dyer's weed (*Sarothamnus Scoparius*) to give the yellow component of green with Indigo. Woad (*Isatis Tinctoria*) was unobtainable, but we have found that Woad, Indigo or even synthetic indigo give identical blue dyes and the colour has not been affected. In addition Julie Douglas writes: 'I have used onion skins (*Allium Cepa*) with dyer's weed. Onions were such a ubiquitious part of the medieval diet and provide a useful, bright and fairly fast dye that I find it hard to accept that they were not added to yellow dye vats. Dyeing with plant dyes requires the use of the same amount of plant weight for weight as cloth. There is a wide range of plants which produce yellow dyes and I suggest that it would have been likely that many dyers would have used a "cocktail" of whichever yellow dyes were available at the time ...'.

His underwear and coif were made of fairly coarse tabby-woven linen. Natural brown tabby-woven cloth from Manx Loughton sheep was used for the hose. All stitches used - running, whipping, backstitch, blanket/buttonhole and top stitch, and the use of narrow strips of cloth as facings for necklines, etc. - can be provenanced to this period. Unbleached linen thread was used for all stitching except for the *huke* and hood, which were sewn with two-ply dyed woollen thread.

(**Above**) From the Conquest to the 16th century hoods were worn by one and all. In bad weather, with an attached cape to protect the shoulders, it is immensely practical and warm; slipped off the head, it provides a bulky scarf around the neck. It can be rolled up to form a hat, or even a bag to carry things in. From the 13th century it was the daily wear of peasant, worker and traveller. Its colours could identify the wearer's political allegiance, guild, or military company. It could hide the hunter in the forest or the face of an assassin in the alley. In the rough game of 'Blindman's Buff' or 'Hoodman Blind' (not then considered too childish for soldiers) one player reversed his hood and the others knotted theirs into clubs to 'buffet' him.

For these photos two hoods were made, one plain and one 'dagged'. The fashion for cutting multi-lobed decorative 'leaf'shaped borders appeared under Henry I of England (1100-1135) and, despite frequent sumptuary laws, continued into the 15th century: 'cut work was great in court and towns, both in men's hoods and in their gowns'. Anyone could afford to 'dagge' a border, but the elaborately cut multi-layered borders of rose leaves, flowers, etc., would decorate the sleeves of the rich alone.

(**Right**) Our Flynt archer's bow is yew, and the arrows careful reconstructions based on those shown in the Luttrell Psalter. (Photos Gerry Embleton)

19

(Right) In the 14th and 15th centuries it was common to wear the hood as a hat: the rolled-up face opening pulled down on the head, the tail wrapped around the head and the cape forming a falling coxcomb - a simple way for an off-duty soldier to dress up for a night out! This became stylised into the fashionable *chaperon*, a tailor-made padded roll with a long tail and falling crown which could either be cut with elaborate leaf-shaped 'dags' or left severely plain. In 1432 Philip the Good of Burgundy ordered hoods with padded brims - chaperons - for his bodyguard archers as part of their livery. In the mid-15th century it was almost a uniform headdress for the aristocracy, and was frequently worn with the hanging tail (*tippet* or *liripipe*) wrapped across the shoulders, or with the whole thing slung to hang behind the shoulder, kept in place by the tail tucked into the waist belt in front.

(Left) A *heuke* (*huk, huke*) was an outer garment, a hooded cloak or gown worn by both men and women. But the term could also mean a sort of livery jacket: in 1439 it was worn by archers under Sir James Skidmore of Herefordshire, retained by Sir James Ormond for Richard, Duke of York's expedition to France. Ormond ordered that 'the said James (Skidmore) shall take for himself and his said archers huk of my said lord the duk, paying for them like as other souldiers of their degree do'. When Joan of Arc was captured she was wearing a cloth-of-gold 'huque … opened on all sides'. This was clearly a tabard-like garment - as was the 'jagged (dagged) huke of black sengle' in Sir John Fastolfe's Wardrobe in 1459. The term is used for a herald's garment in 1295. This example, of wool dyed orange/red with madder (*Rubia Tinctorum*), is a sort of 'poncho' worn by an early 14th century archer. He wears his hood as a hat, and carries his bow covered. (Photo Gerry Embleton)

14th Century Knights

Crests made from parchment, leather, wood and other light materials seem to date from soon after the development of closed helmets. The earliest English representation is the fan-shaped crest on the seal of King Richard I (1189-1199). They both identified the wearer and offered an opportunity for peacock display. For tournaments they reached the heights of fantasy, not always following the wearer's heraldic devices. In combat their use declined, giving way to plumes and smaller ornaments - a golden ball, perhaps set with jewels, was popular in the 15th century. Most common soldiers' helmets were unadorned, except for an occasional twisted scarf wrapped round like a turban or, rarely, a feather; richly equipped household guards might display jewelled mounts and plumes. Burgundian and French officers occasionally wore small helmet pennons marked with numbers indicating their units. (Photo David Lazenby, Middelaldercentret)

(Right) A knight of the 14th century displaying personal heraldry on his shield, saddle and horse bardings. It is not clear when the identifying colours and devices which individual knights displayed on their banners or had painted on their shields began to develop into a more complex system of family heraldry. The adoption of hereditary devices probably began in the middle of the 12th century. At first the charges were simple geometric shapes, animals or objects; these developed, by the 15th century, into the immensely complicated science of heraldry. Small differences in a basic design could indicate different positions within a family, or its different branches. All kinds of symbols were adopted, which might be worn as distinguishing badges by the knight's household and followers. (Photo David Lazenby, Middelaldercentret)

Bright and Shining

Light rain, damp air, even the wearer's perspiration - and by evening bright iron armour has a red bloom of rust. If it takes a grip the armour will cease to function properly. Armour was valuable, and its appearance a matter of prestige; there are many references to its being cleaned - with pumice and olive oil - and polished to a glorious shine. The author has twice been privileged to see the original surface of plate armour, in tiny sections hidden under other parts and so protected for centuries from the ferocious cleaning which has altered the surface of nearly all museum armours; it was exactly like an immensely hard modern steel mirror. For protection armour was sometimes tinned (a Dover inventory of 1361 mentions tinned bascinets), blued, browned, left blackened from the forge, or painted.

Mail is difficult to keep clean: if too lightly oiled it rusts in storage, if too heavily it collects dust and smothers the clothing in greasy dirt. Mail shirts were rolled around in a sack of sand and vinegar (1296), or simply in a barrel of sand.

(Below) Although those liable to be called for military service were responsible for equipping themselves, large scale commercial production was well established by the 13th century; one example will suffice. To equip Philip IV of France's fleet in 1295 an agent purchased at an annual fair 6,309 shields, 2,853 helmets, 4,511 padded jackets, 751 pairs of gauntlets, 1,374 gorgerins and arm braces, 5,067 'iron plates'; 1,885 crossbows and 666,258 quarrels, 13,495 lances or spearheads, 1,989 axes and 14,599 swords and daggers. By the 15th century production flourished on an industrial scale - e.g., in 1427 Milanese armourers equipped 4,000 cavalry and 2,000 infantry in a few days. (Photo David Lazenby, Middelaldercentret)

(Opposite) Plate 3: Head and Neck Defences, c1250 to c1370

(A) The earliest mention of plate neck defences dates from the end of the 13th century; and this effigy of Don Alvero de Cabrera, c1314, is the earliest representation. The collar fits snugly around the neck and chin; together with his padded mail *coif* it would have provided a solid support for a 'great helm'. (Pamplona Cathedral)

(B) The steel collar would also protect the throat and lower part of the face if worn with a kettle hat, a popular style in Spain.

(C) This French knight of c1333 clearly shows a heavily padded mail coif and a small steel cap to form a foundation for the helm. The buttoned sleeves of a finely padded *aketon* are visible beneath a mail shirt; the plate *rondels* must be laced to the mail at the elbows.

(D) The funerary brass of the chevalier Mahiu de Montmorency, c1360, shows a very substantial mail collar. Like the steel collar, it would serve to keep the helm away from the face. (Tavergny, France)

(E) The brass of Sir Miles Stapleton, c1364, shows an *aventail* - a curtain of mail suspended from the helmet rim and fitting around the face. Its form here suggests a rigidly padded mail collar beneath; this 'bullet-shaped' profile, common at this time, is not consistent with wearing a loose, unlined, hanging mail aventail. (Formerly at Ingham, Sussex)

(F) The brass of Sir Hugh Hastyngs, c1347, shows very solid neck defences. Note also that D, E & F have body and thigh defences of fabric or leather with rivets, indicating plates beneath. These sort of constructions lasted in use well into the 15th century. (Elsing, Norfolk)

(G) Some padded body defences worn by common soldiers in sources of this time show the same kind of 'free-standing' protective collars. (Maciejowski Bible, French, c1250)

(H) Bascinet with movable 'nasal visor', c1350 - a transitional style between the classic nasal helmet and the visored helmet. Double locking pins kept the nasal in place; nevertheless, the padding and firm seating of helmet and aventail must have been crucial - a blow across the nasal would surely smash it into the wearer's teeth. (Extant example, Schweizerisches Landesmuseum, Zurich)

(I) A wall painting commemorating the funeral of Bernabo Visconti, Milan, c1370, shows a quilted jack or arming doublet, to be worn alone or beneath a mail shirt, and a *klappvisier* worn with an obviously padded aventail.

(J) The padded aventail was fastened to the helmet by a cord, running through short tubes which were fixed to the helmet and passed through slots in the aventail's leather border.

(K) The effigy of Albrecht von Hohenlohe at Sconthal Church, c1319, closely associates the images of his bascinet and helm.

(L) German or north Italian visored bascinet, c1370; this was a popular and relatively practical war helmet.

(M) *Klappvisier*, c1370, now in the Musée Valaria, Sitten/Sion, Switzerland.

A B C D E F G H I J K L M

(**Opposite**) Two fashionable knights of the latter half of the 14th century wear helms decorated for the tournament, and virtually complete plate armour - some hidden beneath rich fabric, some supplemented with mail (see Plate 4, page 27). The small *bascinet* was worn either beneath the 'great helm' or alone - note that the left hand example has fittings for a removable visor.

Decoration and military display were vitally important, not only to identify the individual and attract attention to his valorous deeds, but also to advertise his success in a harshly competitive world. Display meant wealth; wealth meant power; power attracted new allies and protegés, and deterred potential enemies and rebels. Household account books list very large sums spent on decoration - for banners, tents, pennons, even for the sails of ships. A mixture of embroidery, painting and appliqué was frequently used on heraldic devices.

In 1352 some 330 standards were painted and appliquéd for Edward III of England; 250 of them, each requiring 2½ yards of worsted and 1½ yards of linen,

were painted vermilion and azur, and 80 of yellow and blue worsted were painted with leopards and fleurs-de-lys. Eighteen painters worked for 12 days, and 50 other workers for nearly a month, sewing and treating them with candle wax. The king's surcoat in 1345-49 was made of 1¼ yards each of blue and red cloth and 1½ yards of yellow for lions rampant and fleurs-de-lys. In 1351-52, 150 of King Edward's archers were supplied with *courtepys*, a task which employed 15 men for 12 days at a cost of 4¼ pence each per day.

In 1352 a tent of deep blue was ordered for Edward, ornamented with stars and crowns in yellow worsted, and another of green lined red, powdered with yellow worsted eagles. In 1386, during Franco-Burgundian preparations for an invasion of England, the ducal painter Melchior Broederlam decorated banners with the duke's coat of arms, and the sail of his ship with his motto in letters of gold. (Photo David Lazenby, Middelaldercentret)

(**Above**) A 14th century gun crew fire their bombard under the protection of a mantlet, covered with wet hides to protect it from fire-arrows. The kettle hats of the crew were very practical during siege warfare, allowing clear all-round vision and good protection against the plunging flight of arrow and bolt.

The echoing thunder of guns and the bitter smell of powder smoke were doing more than just frightening horses - castle walls were cracking under their bombardment. Modern experiments have proved that the old siege engines such as *trebuchets* were more accurate

and destructive than has sometimes been assumed; but this new weapon would decisively tilt the balance of advantage against the defenders of fortified towns and castles. In open field battles massed archers were already challenging the dominance of the mounted knight; over the next century other types of disciplined infantry, manoeuvring and fighting *en masse*, would change the necessary composition of armies and alter the relative fortunes of the military classes. (Photo David Lazenby, Middelaldercentret)

(Opposite) Plate 4: 14th Century Gambesons, Pourpoints, Jupons & Coat Armour

(Above) Who was the common soldier? He was one of hundreds of thousands of individuals each with a life of his own to lead. He might come from a village, a town, or - less often - from a city. He might be a rootless traveller, a hardened criminal, a bored craftsman or small tradesman seeking adventure, a runaway apprentice, or a dutiful servant of his local lord or his king. He might be fulfilling his legal obligations alongside his neighbours, fleeing the plough to seek glory, or following dark dreams of loot and rape. He might be a professional, a well-paid veteran of several campaigns with money already clinking in his purse; or a bewildered peasant levy, left behind sick and starving in a ditch during a hard retreat.

For some it was a career with promise. Sir Robert Knollys from Cheshire may originally have been a common archer, as perhaps was Sir Hugh Calverly. Rough-and-ready Robert Lewer started as a common soldier, and rose in service under Edward II to be constable of Oldham Castle. In a time of frequent wars a man's fortunes rose and fell; Lewer died an executed rebel in 1323. We know that one Colpin - 'a very valiant man although from humble stock' - rose to command 300 Englishmen in the Burgundian army, and prospered until killed by a cannon shot at Nancy in 1477.

Other than the weapons and armour he was supposed to bring to war, and perhaps the coat or suit of clothes issued by his town or master, the soldier's 'equipment' did not extend much beyond those personal possessions which he could carry on the march: a purse, an eating knife, spoon, bowl, clothes, underwear and shoes, cloak and bedding brought from home. Normally travelling in small groups to an army's rendezvous, soldiers might share cooking pots, rations and a few tools - and perhaps even a cart or packhorse for the lucky. (Photo David Lazenby, Middelaldercentret)

These 14th-century terms for the defensive fabric garments worn with some types of armour cannot be clearly defined. Medieval man's free, apparently interchangeable and contradictory use of such words defeats our modern passion for assigning everything to exact categories.

(A) St George, from a late 14th century manuscript. He wears a quilted *gambeson*, perhaps over plate defences which give him the typical 'hourglass' silhouette of the knight of this period. Note the sloping line of his *aventail* from helmet to shoulder. Without a padded lining the mail would hang vertically from the base of the neck, providing little protection.

(B) Tomb effigy of Walter von Hohenklingen, killed by the Swiss at Sempach, 1386. His pointed *bascinet* has the visor removed. The quilted fabric- or leather-covered aventail is probably interlined with mail, of which the 'dagged' edge is visible. He wears a breastplate, with lance rest on the right side, over a full-sleeved padded gambeson, which follows fashionable form and is probably worn over a mail shirt. Note the large tailored sleeves, and the 'hourglass' plate gauntlets. Many combinations of padded defence, plate armour and mail were worn at this time by both knights and their followers.

In the Historical Museum in Lucerne, Switzerland, is a mail shirt worn by Duke Leopold III of Austria captured at Sempach. It is an amazing piece of tailoring in iron, which follows the fashionable lines of Hohenklingen's gambeson; three different sizes of rings are used in its construction.

(C) This figure of St George is a perfect example of the appearance of the knight at the end of the 14th century. He wears the very widely used *Hundsgugel* or 'dog-faced' bascinet, its aventail tied down to shoulders and breast with 'points' - laces. This must have been a normal practice, and since mail is extremely flexible it would not restrict movement unduly.

One surviving *Hundsgugel* bascinet at Churburg in the Tyrol bears a splendid Latin quotation from St Luke: 'But he walked straight through them all and went away…'

(D) Reconstruction of the heavily padded interior of the aventail, a detail clearly visible on the tomb effigy of Duke Philip the Bold of Burgundy, now in the Musée des Beaux-Arts, Dijon.

(E, F & G) The *pourpoint* of Charles de Blois, pretender to the duchy of Brittany, killed at Avray in 1364. Its once beautifully patterned fabric is now faded; but note that its silhouette follows that of figure C. The buttons are probably of wood covered with silk.

(H) The coat armour (or *jupon*, or pourpoint, or doublet?) of King Charles VI of France, dating from the end of the 14th century and now preserved in Chartres Cathedral. It is of quilted white linen stuffed with cotton wool and covered with crimson silk damask. In the left side are two slits for the suspension straps of a sword scabbard.

Both of these garments have domed buttons above the waist line, and flat ones below. There is some disagreement among historians as to whether they should be regarded as 'civilian' or 'military' garments.

14th Century Women on Campaign

Women usually accompanied medieval armies - as sutlers, serving women, wives, laundresses and prostitutes. Sometimes their presence was harshly controlled (Henry V of England ordered that anyone who found a whore in camp could take her money, drive her off and break her arm). At other times they were tolerated in considerable numbers, and could be recruited as a general labour force. At the siege of Neuss by the Burgundians in 1475 some 4,000 camp women marched to the sound of trumpets and pipes, with a banner given by Charles the Bold, to work on a canal to divert the Rhine.

More rarely, women of the land-holding classes actually led troops in fulfilment of the family's feudal duty, or fought alongside brother or husband - or in place of a husband lost or imprisoned. Women of any class might play an important part in the defence of a castle or town. We know of at least one who served as a common soldier, known to be a woman by her comrades but looking and behaving tough enough to pass as a man. In battle some wore men's clothes and even armour - but these were the rare exceptions.

Most women made the camp a more comfortable place, cooked food and nursed the sick. Like their men, they would have dressed to suit their station in life and the hardships to be encountered. A woman of the aristocracy would have lived like the knight who was her husband, relative or protector, with spacious tents, comfortable camp equipage and plentiful servants. The humblest soldier's woman would have shared his cloak in a barn or under a hedge. The prettiest of fashionable dresses, the most frivolous of headdresses would have been very rarely seen. No one went campaigning in a party frock.

(**Opposite**) The scene that might have greeted a weary 14th century captain, home after a hard day of drill and organisation. He has brought his wife along on this safe stage of the campaign and they have found billets in a merchant's house, suitable to their status. His wife rises at the clatter of his horse on the cobbles outside and the bustle of their servants and his archer guard. He will wash off the grime and sweat, change into a comfortable gown and share a supper with her. They will discuss their days' work in detail - his under arms, hers running his household. She was raised to this world, and her grasp of kinship politics and understanding of most military matters will calm him. How good she looks in fine bleached linen, and a simple gown of the very finest English wool woven in Flanders, dyed at Prato near Florence - expensive, but worth it to give such pleasure.
(Photo David Lazenby, Middelaldercentret)

(**Right**) Meanwhile, out in the fringe of the woods the wife of a *vintainer* - the commander of 20 men - gathers wood for her cooking, breathing the evening air away from the smoke and noise of the camp and planning her soup. Her husband has found his soldiers billets in a sprawling farm. Life is always hard, but not so bad with her ox of a husband, a sensible and much respected man who always goes home from his campaigning with money in his purse - sometimes a surprising amount. This his fifth campaign and his wife's second. She has born him five children, but three died in infancy; her surviving girls were both married and gone before they were 16, so there is nothing to keep her at home.

(**Below & right**) She wears a yellow kirtle - underdress - which she made and dyed herself. Her overdress is a woad-dyed gown her husband 'found' for her. She takes pleasure in the fashionable buttoned sleeves and the close fit allowed by the several panels of the body.

The patterns for these garments were based on those found at Herjolfness in Greenland at the beginning of the 20th century. They are meticulously reconstructed using vegetable-dyed wool, linen thread, and only the sewing techniques known to have been used at the time. The narrow panels of the torso of the dress are shaped to follow the body's form, not to economise, though there is nothing to indicate that this gown belonged to a 'rich' woman. The buttoned sleeves are typical of the 14th century. Note the two methods of shortening the skirt length for convenience when working: by tucking up the front, and by gathering some of the length over a second belt worn on the hips. (Photos Anne Embleton, reconstruction Julie Douglass)

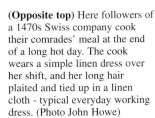

(**Opposite top**) Here followers of a 1470s Swiss company cook their comrades' meal at the end of a long hot day. The cook wears a simple linen dress over her shift, and her long hair plaited and tied up in a linen cloth - typical everyday working dress. (Photo John Howe)

(**Opposite**) Little jewellery was worn, but the belts worn by all classes seem to have made up for any lack of decoration elsewhere. Here are two beautifully reconstructed 14th century belt buckles: prized purchases - or loot - for any young soldier, and a fine gift for a buxom cook … (Photos & reconstructions Simon Metcalfe)

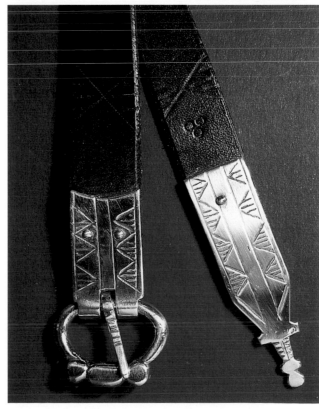

(Opposite) Plate 5: Underwear and Basic Civilian Costume

To understand how costume works we must know what was worn under it, and the social customs connected with wearing it. The basic undergarments of civilian and soldier alike were the same until the first issue of military underwear in the 19th century. They consisted of underpants (*braies*), stockings (*chausses*) and a shirt (Latin *camisia*, Norman *chemise*, Anglo-Saxon *smock*).

At first braies were an important garment, almost like trousers, tucked into stocking-like hose. By the 14th century the hose had become tight-fitting separate 'trouserlegs' which were laced at the thigh to a jacket-like doublet. During the 15th century they became one trouser-like garment supported by lacing to the doublet. At the end of the century they were cut higher above the hipbone and became self-supporting. For physical labour or relaxing in warm weather the doublet would be unfastened at the chest and thrown back with the sleeves hanging (see page 53). Most of the following examples are taken from non-military sources, but all apply equally to the soldier and his followers.

(A) The tunic, the basic male garment from the earliest medieval times. Initially a shirt-like garment which was pulled on over the head, this became more or less tailored to shape as the centuries passed. The simple primary colours shown in early manuscripts may owe more to the artists' palette than to actual fabrics; but it appears that there was a love of bright colours, in applied decorative bands or overall patterns. We know, for instance, that a Saxon nobleman presented to Ely Abbey a tunic of red and purple interwoven across the shoulders and heavily embroidered in gold. (Bronze font, Hildersheim Cathedral, c1210)

(B to I) These illustrations from various sources show the development of braies and hose. At first the braies resemble light trousers (B), slit at the bottom so that they can be tied comfortably round the ankle (C), tied up at the knee (H), or to the waist (E, F). The waist is rolled over a belt or cord, sometimes with a suspended purse (G) worn safely out of sight under the tunic. Stocking-like hose are worn at first to the knee, and later to mid-thigh, tied up to the waistband (I).

(J) Although they usually slept naked, medieval men are rarely shown stripped to the waist for work; instead, they took off their hose and worked in their shirts and underpants - as in this mid-15th century French illustration of a harvester, with the skirts of his shirt tucked up into his belt.

(K & L) This 15th century source shows shirts with unusual features: deep side slits, back slits and square neck openings. Since 15th century fashions rarely exposed the shirt it was usually cut along the simplest T-shaped lines with a slit opening at the neck. The author has found no 15th century references to drawstring fastenings at neck or wrists.

(M) Typical 15th century underpants based on several illustrations: left, the commonest style (Ducal Palace, Dijon); right, 'bikini' pants with side ties - far less common, these do appear in some Swiss-German and Italian sources. Tiny black ones appear in some manuscript illustrations, but may have been added to nude figures by later, more prudish hands.

(N) Reconstructions based on several contemporary illustrations.

(O) Reconstruction of a typical man's or woman's shirt, with gussets under the arms and inserted to widen the skirts.

(P) One of the Duke of Berry's Books of Hours shows a good example of a woman's everyday working dress, suitable for any camp follower. It is hitched up and bunched over the waist belt to shorten the skirt, with the front also folded up and tucked into the belt. Separate long sleeves might be pinned on.

(Q) Reconstruction of the long-skirted doublet and separate-legged hose typical of the late 14th-early 15th centuries.

(R) Front view of the same, from a drawing by Montagna. Details of shirt collars, late 15th century, from:

(S) Pietro di Domenico,

(T) Piero della Francesca, and

(U) Piero di Cosimo.

(V) Landsknecht shirt with its normally gathered collar loosened. At the end of the 15th century the shirt became increasingly visible, so more attention was paid to making it decorative.

(W) Two 'ladies' who followed the armies, drawn by Urs Graf, c1516-25. The previously hidden and humble shirt has now become an important part of high - and not so high - fashion.

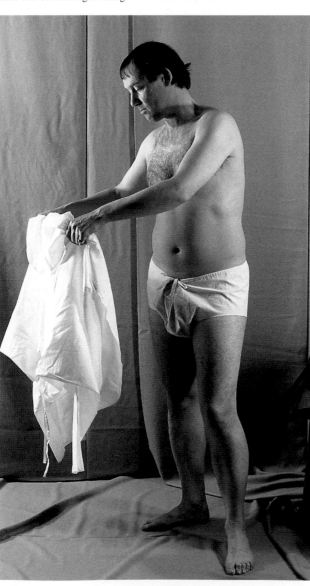

(Left) Basic masculine undergarments during the 14th and 15th centuries consisted of shirt and braies (underpants), usually of linen. (Photo John Howe)

From the 4th century to the 12th a loose smock-like tunic, varying in length and detail, was by far the commonest outer garment for all classes. The earliest were cut along simple geometric lines, and except for periodic fashions for tighter fitting garments - notably during the 12th century - little attempt was made to fit the clothes to the body until the 14th. The 15th century saw an increasing interest in tailoring, and towards the end of the century almost skin-tight hose and doublets were the rage. Tight-fitting, high-waisted hose and bulky sleeves gave way to the 'square' look in the early 16th century (see Plates 10 & 11, pages 89-91).

A

B

C

D

E

F

G

H

I

J

K

L

M

N

O

P

Q

R

S

T

U

V

W

(Above & right) Over the shirt and braies were worn woollen hose, cut as tight as the material allowed; these are 15th century one-piece hose with integral feet.

Over the hose, with their modest codpiece, is worn a tight-fitting black doublet to which the hose are attached by metal-tipped laces ('points').

Over these goes a red 'coat' or jacket - in this case fashionably short and pleated, of a style popular with soldiers as well as young bloods.

Finally, depending upon circumstance, season and pocket, a woollen gown might cover the whole ensemble. A common soldier would rarely have one as long and well-fitting as this splendid example. Shorter gowns of many styles were popular cold weather wear for soldier and civilian alike; but one can imagine that any soldier 'finding' an elegant gown like this, unsuited to the workaday world, would be tempted to sell it on to those with the money and leisure to enjoy it. (Photos John Howe)

15th Century Men's Costume

(**Opposite**) The everyday working dress of the soldier cannot be understood without knowledge of contemporary civilian dress, a version of which was worn by all soldiers. The weight of cloth, the way it was cut and fitted together changed over time, but clothes for war and work have always been basically practical. What may seem like bizarre 'fancy dress' to modern eyes turns out, when properly reconstructed and tested, to be at least as comfortable as the modern equivalent. (But make a careless mistake or a short-cut in your reconstruction, and you will end up with something that restricts movement and is unrealistically uncomfortable.)

We should not imagine that soldiers were generally ragged and dirty. Those who followed a rich lord were doubtless well looked after, and campaigns that reduced men to scarecrows were comparatively rare. Armies collected a 'tail' of followers; camp women would have made 'running repairs', and merchants and tinkers were actively encouraged to come into camp to sell necessities and luxuries to the soldiery. After victories looted clothing, including gaudy finery, was doubtless mixed with practical everyday wear.

(**Right**) Garrison life could be comfortable, and many a man retained in the service of a lord would have spent much of his time dressed like this 1470s Swedish soldier in Savoyard service. He wears a comfortably long livery coat of good quality woollen cloth 'fulled' to give it a felt-like appearance, with hose, a dagged hood with a long liripipe, and a cap. He shows off his relatively prosperous position by the ornaments on his dagger, belt and long sword, and his concern with fashion by his long hair. Eating grapes from the local vineyard, he has the air of one enjoying a 'cushy number'. (Photo Gerry Embleton)

(Above) The finely gilded brass fittings on belt, sword hilt and chape were a gift, and he is justly proud of them; but he is a professional soldier, paid well to protect his employer. He has studied with a pupil of Tallhoffer in Stuttgart and knows how to use his elegant sword to deadly effect. He takes great pleasure in exercising with it, and always remembers a quotation his master passed on to him, from a work written a hundred years before:

'He does not do it for fighting, but to have deeper breath: and it is a certain thing that one is fitter and more erect and much straighter for it - all these good things come from fencing'. (Photos Gerry Embleton)

Headgear and Footwear

(Opposite top) Many kinds of hats were worn by soldiers: all the different felt and woollen types based on narrow or shallow cone shapes, with or without the edge partly or fully turned up; stocking caps; rolled tubes of cloth; hoods rolled into hats; and broad-brimmed straw hats in summer. There was no specifically military headgear;

consideration was that it had to be put somewhere when a helmet was worn, either inside the helmet or packed away. (Photos left, David Lazenby, Middel-aldercentret; right, John Howe)
(Below & opposite below) Stout footwear was essential for the footsoldier. Most medieval footwear was made by sewing soft moccasin-like soles and uppers together, inside out, and then turning the shoe right side out; thicker outer soles could be added afterwards. Heavily constructed

ankle boots (called 'cockers' in England) were popular with peasants and travellers. These were laced, buckled, or closed with points or a wrap-around strap. Many had thick soles and heels and some had nailed soles, although concrete evidence is surprisingly scarce beyond a written mention or two and a couple of illustrations. William Langland (c1360-1399) described 'knobbed' or nailed shoes in *The Vision Concerning Piers Plowman* - 'knoppede schon clouted ful thykke'. Many a soldier must have come equipped with shoes like these - or must have searched for a pair among the dead on the battlefield.

A horse, and good pay, would have allowed a fashion-minded soldier to sport pointed shoes; but very long ones - like the 'crackowes' named after Cracow in Poland, and popular during the reign of Richard II (1377-1399) and in the mid- to late 15th century - would have been worn on campaign by only the most eccentric dandy, and then only on horseback or in camp. Combat quickly discovers whether fashions are practical or not.

Long boots were popular and practical for riding, made rough and short-toed for hard service, or of finest leather, tight-fitting, with elegantly pointed toes for the fashionable. These were made wide enough at the shin to allow the foot to pass comfortably; then the surplus leather was folded back to the outside of the foot and leg, and secured with hooks and eyes or buckles and straps. Illustrations suggest that wonderfully elastic and supple leathers were used to achieve a stocking-like fit, but our ignorance of the techniques employed makes convincing reconstructions extremely difficult.

The longest boots had turned-down cuffs at mid-thigh, and a strap pierced with holes was attached on the outer edge to be tied to points at the wearer's waist or on the thigh of his hose. Boots were frequently lined, at substantial extra cost. Half-boots were very popular too, for walking as well as riding. Burgundian mounted archers, who needed to do both with ease, were specifically ordered to wear ones with rounded toes. (Photos, left to right: Gerry Embleton, Anne Embleton, John Howe, John Howe)

15th Century Women's Costume

An army had few 'professional' women followers. Most were those who temporarily attached themselves for profit, those young and tough enough to go adventuring with the lads, those married or 'connected' who followed their men - and those less fortunate who clung to the army's outer rim, desperately trying to survive as it cut a swathe through their land, homes and lives.

Women lived and worked hard in villages and towns - ran their own homes, spun, wove and sewed their families' clothes, grew and cooked food, ran farms and businesses, and worked in the crafts and guilds (and as labourers). Their dress would have reflected their background and circumstances, just as it did the men's.

Sometimes they took an active part in the wars; we have many 15th century references, but this example from a century earlier shows just how important their participation could be. In 1292 the city of Zurich was weakened by a costly war with Winterthur in which many of their men had fallen. Duke Albrecht of Austria sought to take advantage of the situation and moved with a powerful army to take the city. The women of Zurich put on armour and took up their menfolk's weapons. They gathered in the Müsterhof armed with spear and shield and, led by one Hedwig ab Burghalden, paraded with fife and drum across Zurich's bridges and around the walls, shouting and brandishing their weapons. Duke Albrecht, believing that the town was full of soldiers and having no stomach for a hard fight or siege, made peace with Zurich and withdrew. (Photos David Lazenby, Middelaldercentret)

These three women wear everyday dress typical of the southern Germans or Swiss, c1470.

(Above left) A blue underdress of thin wool or linen, cut with tight sleeves just wide enough to pass the hand through. This example is laced up the front and on both sides of the bodice, a practical design allowing (as in this case) the width of the bodice to be adjusted during pregnancies.

(Above centre) This example shows the same basic cut but with a lower neckline showing more of the chemise. The skirt was very full and if cut 'on the cross' - i.e. with warp and weft running diagonally - the cloth falls in graceful conical folds.

(Above right) This lady has dressed up to go out or receive guests. Over her sage green underdress she wears a blue woollen gown, lined with 'murray' (mulberry colour). The gown is almost identical to the underdress, but cut fuller, to be pulled on over it. She has pinned a narrow band to her headcloth, which falls gracefully over her shoulder. This would be pinned across the chin when going out. (Photos Philippe Krauer, l'Illustré)

(Right) A woman's 'crowning glory' was usually worn plaited and pinned up in various ways. Frequent combing was necessary to keep it free of parasites, and this must have been a common sight around camp and castle.

Like so many other things women's headdress was subject to local custom and courtly fashion. It seems that married women and widows kept their hair covered and others could show it, but there were many exceptions. A simple rectangle of cloth covered the head, sometimes pinned up as a veil (which could also be a separate item). Fashions for headbands, small caps, flowing hair and plaits came and went. A soldier's woman would have dressed for travelling or a normal working day, and when out of doors the head was usually covered.

(Left) Hoods that buttoned under the chin were popular in the 15th and 16th centuries, and a plain red or black hood left open in front of the neck was widely worn by French, Burgundian and English countrywomen - and no doubt by many soldiers' companions.

(Below) Wooden clogs - 'pattens' - were commonly worn to keep both aristocratic and peasant feet out of the mud, but were not suitable for long marches. (Photos Gerry Embleton)

(Left) Head cloths might be of cheap, coarse linen, of expensive silk, or even of 'cloths of fyne gold all about your head' (13th century). Many elaborate styles developed, but the exigencies of campaigning would dictate a certain simplicity at any period. On high days and holidays the headdress might blossom into one of the many elaborate displays currently popular.

During the 14th and 15th centuries these developed into various regional styles of headdress, and finally into the close-fitting caps of the 16th century - and the headdress of many folk costumes of the 19th century. (Photo John Howe)

(Right) In the Swiss chronicles of the 1470s we find a fashion among southern German and Swiss women for a false fringe in coloured wool worn at the nape of the neck, in red, blue, green, red or blue and white, or green and yellow. (Photo Gerry Embleton)

15th Century Italian Soldiers

The basic elements of costume were common across Europe, but soldiers from each country displayed local peculiarities. Paintings from northern Italy - a centre of fine cloth production and of trade with the eastern Mediterranean - show a certain stylishness and richness of colour. 14th and 15th century Italy saw a liking for well-fitted clothes, *mi-parti* colours, and the early introduction of slashes at elbow and shoulder to aid movement in tight clothing. Armour style was of the rounded 'Italian Gothic' form, *barbutes* and small *sallets* being more popular than kettle hats. Light armour with brigandines, greaves and mail sleeves was common. Many church wall paintings include warriors, and apart from a few features they look very much like French or Burgundians. Italy produced many mercenary bands employed throughout Europe as well as by rival cities at home, and generally they appear to have been well, even richly turned out.

(**Opposite**) This 15th century Italian soldier keeping a gate of his master's house in peacetime wears comfortable everyday clothes, his only weapon a glaive. Understandably, lighter clothing was popular, like this sleeveless doublet, and loose tabards were frequently worn against the cool of evening or to show heraldic arms. His belt and buckles are typically Italian.

(**Below**) Hose soled with leather were popular in the 14th and 15th centuries and appear to be particularly so in Italy. Soldiers are shown wearing them in battle, but they would not have stood up to a long march.
(Photos Gerry Embleton)

Ducal troops might wear splendid heraldic tabards and elaborately patterned hose, and there are a few references to identifying colours and badges: 50% of the advance payment made to Neapolitan mercenaries in 1451 came in the form of cloth - red, blue, green, white and purple. Sigismondo Malatesta's men wore his and his mistress's entwined initials, S and I. At the end of the 15th century the commander of 400 Florentine troops ordered for each a white doublet, red and white hose, a white cap, shoes, armour and pikes, some with handguns - 'the most beautiful thing which has ever been ordered for the city of Florence'.

(**Above**) Italian women, even when accompanying a foreign army, would have worn touches of their own local costume - not the elaborate dresses shown in religious paintings, but the simple styles shown in more secular illustrations.
(Photo Gerry Embleton).

Cloth and Dyes: The Possible and the Permissible

In recent years a great deal of progress has been made in the study of textiles. It is now recognised that the blackened scraps which archaeologists used to scrape off brooches and jewellery to get at the metal are actually evidence which can tell us about the weaves and material of the fabrics which lay beneath them.

It comes as a shock to see the fine quality and sophistication of even the very earliest surviving fragments when cleaned and conserved. The patterned surfaces and glowing colours look remarkably 'modern', even with textiles woven and dyed as long as 2,000 to 3,000 years ago. Mediaeval textile finds suggest highly developed weaves and beautiful colours, stripes and patterns. We also find many imported cloths and silks from the East; but most of the common soldier's clothes - and his superiors', too - would have been made out of woollen cloth. There was nothing crude about the material produced at domestic or commercial level, however. By the 15th century the

revenues from the trade in woollen cloth supported many a European noble; and we should never make the mistake of assuming that our ancestors were any less expert at employing the technologies of their day than we are with our own.

Underwear, shirts and some clothing was made of cotton, linen, hemp, nettle, fur and felt. Many vegetable dyes were used - the most important being Woad (blues), Madder (reds), and Weld (yellows), which give a wide range of subtle and sometimes surprisingly bright colours. Neither were these solely the prerogative of the rich: the poorest Scottish Highland families produced their tartans, the poorest peasants have found ways to add colours to their clothes, and the humblest of common soldiers have gone to their deaths gaudily dressed. Some medieval colours frequently mentioned are not identifiable today: 'pluncket', for example, is not known; and 'russet' appears to have been either a reddish brown or grey.

(Above) An Italian footsoldier in a deep *barbutta* helmet and Italian-style gauntlets, c1465. (Below) A mild Italian influence could be seen in those parts of Switzerland and France which shared a frontier with Savoy and what is now Italy, visible in the clothes and equipment of these two very 'modern' Savoyard soldiers, c1470. They wear the cross of Savoy, white on red, and simple Milanese helmets. One leans on a pole axe and the other is armed with the very latest type of handgun. Northern Italy produced some of the finest woollen cloth, and these soldiers appear to have benefited from employment by a lord whose castle sits profitably on the trade route between Italy and the blossoming Burgundian empire. (Photos John Howe)

Sumptuary Laws

There were frequent attempts by crown and church to control the richness of dress, to curb extravagance and to keep each class and degree firmly in its place on the hierarchical ladder. Cloth, cut, colour and trimmings were carefully described for each class and forbidden to those below. Sometimes the laws lapsed; sometimes they were reinforced. How effective they were is open to debate - probably less and less the further one travelled from the court's influence. The spread of displays of wealth downwards through the classes occurs particularly when money is flowing toward groups which lack relative political power, and

this was certainly true of the 15th century merchant class.

It is interesting to note that Henry IV of England's sumptuary laws of 1403 specifically exempted men-at-arms when in armour, 'who may dress as they please'; and that Edward IV's strict code of 1463 to restrict the wearing of rich apparel seems not to have applied to the soldiers: '... provided also, that this ordinance do in no wise extend to any manner of array necessarily to be worn in war, or in the feats of the same'. It is doubtful if soldiers paid much attention to sumptuary laws unless under direct royal command or some other unusually strict regime.

Livery

It is usually suggested that military uniform - mass issue of uniformly coloured clothing to soldiers - began in Europe in the 17th century. We have enough earlier evidence of regular and occasional issues on a large scale to challenge that idea. Where we do find reference to soldiers' clothing it is often in the colours of their employer, lord, captain or country. Entire armies wore national liveries and badges, and some town contingents wore uniform clothing from head to foot. There are countless records; here are a few examples:

In 1295 English recruits from Norfolk wore white coats costing 3 shillings each. In 1300 the men of Tournai wore red with a silver castle on breast and back. In 1385 an order was issued that all Scottish soldiers and their French allies were to wear a white St Andrew's cross on breast and back, on a black patch if the surcoat was white. In 1416 crossbowmen from Amiens sent to Abbeville to fight the English wore green and white.

Frequently the arms and armour that each man was expected to possess were exactly laid down, and even if these demands were seldom met it can be argued that at times medieval soldiers must have looked as roughly 'uniform' as their 17th century descendants during the Thirty Years War.

The term 'livery' covered everything given to those who served a lord in exchange for their keep, but livery 'clothing' (a specific 15th century term) was an essential part of such payment. From the swarming entourage of the Lord Chancellor of England to the humblest knight's humblest servant, they were given clothes and badges of a quality and colour that showed their position in the hierarchy, whom they served and whose protection they enjoyed. At the highest level the quality of the cloth and furs used were jealously guarded signs of privilege; at the lowest, the minimum necessary to clothe a man without shaming his master.

Usually the colours and badges were associated with a lord's family or coat of arms, but they could be an individual choice to mark some special occasion such as a marriage or bereavement, or simply because they were the only colours available at the time. In a royal household a positive shower of colourful clothes descended from on high, advertising the king's prosperity and generosity, and 15th century wardrobe accounts list in great detail the cloths and colours. For instance, in 1434/35 King Henry VI of England issued liveries which were predominantly green in summer, but his highest officials wore murray, sanguine and violet. His sergeant-at-arms wore murray and 'good striped Salisbury cloth'. Many of the humbler servants wore a mixture of 'musterdevilers' (a mixed grey-blue) and striped cloth.

Naturally, those closest to a prince received the richest liveries, but for exceptionally important occasions special clothing would be given to much of the court. For example, for the reception of the Emperor Charles IV in 1378, Philip Duke of Burgundy (1364-1404) gave his household black and grey clothing; in 1384, green to welcome the king of France, and red and blue to impress the English negotiators at the talks at Boulogne; in 1385, red for a marriage at Cambrai; in 1389, red and white for the reception of the king once more at Dijon; in 1395, black; green and white for a noble marriage in 1402, and so on.

Liveries were also given to men and woman injured or grown sick in royal service. In 1349 one John de Pasterhaye was awarded 2 pence per day for life and a robe annually 'because he was maimed in the king's service', as was John Helmeswell in 1346.

Great dukes like Philip the Good and Charles the Bold of Burgundy dressed their officers and bodyguards in jewelled helmets, cloth of gold, silver and gold badges and sumptuous gowns. For a meeting with the Emperor in 1473 Charles gave new robes and rich clothing to 1,003 members of his household. His captain of archers received blue velvet for his '*jacquecte*' and white damask for his

(Above) A tough veteran captain in Charles the Bold's Burgundian service, wearing a heavily embroidered version of the ducal livery as laid down in the Abbeville Ordinance, 31 July 1471. (Photo Gerry Embleton)

pourpoint, and 110 of 'my lord's guard of men-at-arms' received *paletots* (livery jackets) and mantles of cloth of gold, cloth of silver and silk and blue velvet, and pourpoints of crimson satin. The Duke of Berry, a vastly wealthy patron of the arts, even had gay clothing issued to villagers so that they might make a pleasing spectacle as he passed by …

Important political and military leaders like the Duke of Warwick made clear statements about their great power when they moved around the country with armed retainers at their backs. In January 1458 he attended the great council of Westminster attended by 600 men in red coats embroidered with his ragged staff badge on breast and back: in an age without mass media, what

better way to announce 'Warwick is here'?

Private armies like these could be an unruly nuisance and a threat to law, order and peace. Kings and great dukes who achieved strong central governments eventually passed laws banning the wearing of livery badges and colours other than their own, and at the end of the 15th century Henry VII all but stamped out private armies in England.

Badges, worn extensively by the 15th century military, were also given in their thousands to civilian supporters (or to attract them) on important occasions. For Richard II's coronation 26,000 fustian boar badges were handed out - half embroidered, half painted.

(**Right**) Simple bi-coloured
livery was frequently adopted by
town contingents - in this case
the black and white of Fribourg,
ally to Berne in the Burgundian
wars, c1476. Livery colours were
also used on equipment; in 1475
a 600-strong contingent from the
imperial city of Lübeck wore
coats halved red and white, and
their 27 wagons were painted in
the same colours. (Photo John
Howe)

(**Below**) One of the English Duke
of Warwick's archers who fought
at Towton, 29 March 1461,
wearing the duke's livery over a
light jack and his own clothes.
(Photo Gerry Embleton)

(**Opposite top**) A soldier serving
the Graf von Thierstein, owner of
the castle of Haute Koenigsbourg
in present-day Alsace, wears the
Thierstein arms on a shield on his
breast and a bi-coloured livery
jacket. This is not an important
castle; the post is a comfortable
one and suits this soldier's
relaxed ways. He is something of
a traveller - note the pilgrim
badges in his hat - and turns to
soldiering when there is nothing
better to do. (Photo Gerry
Embleton)

The Duke of Burgundy's Archer Bodyguard

At this time it was
fashionable to have
bodyguards of archers,
both for protection and display.
The Burgundian dukes lavished
gifts on their bodyguard archers -
not entirely unselfishly. The 40
archiers de corps under their two
captains waited ready and
mounted to accompany him
whenever he moved quarters;
they surrounded their master
wherever he went, day and night,
and stood between him and the
assassin's knife. They were to
practice with their bows
whenever possible, and the ducal
artillery accounts mention bows,
shooting gloves and bracers for
them. They acted like a modern
president's motorcycle outriders,
and also at times acted as
'police', going without their
bows to control over-enthusiastic
crowds.

In 1416 the duke had 24 robes
made for them, embroidered on
each sleeve with three sheaves of
arrows. In 1433 they were issued
with black and grey cloth to
make 29 '*heuques ytaliennes*'
embroidered with gold; these
were open at the sides like a
herald's tabard. In 1435 there
was an issue of *paletots* in grey
and black with the initials of
Duke Philip and his duchess
embroidered in gold and silver
thread. In 1442 their captain 'le
seigneur de Ternant' was paid 42
livres to repair their jacks; the
captain wore a paletot
embroidered with gold. In 1452
we read of the archers taking off
their jacks and going in their
pourpoints to be lighter (perhaps
what is worn in the two Schilling
illustrations described below). In
1465 we read of black and violet
livery, with a white cross of
Burgundy, firesteel, flint and
sparks embroidered (see page 51,
Plate 7, item B). In 1467 Jehen
de Moncheauix, 'plumetier',
supplied plumes to the captain
and archers. In 1471 they were to
wear jacks with high collars
instead of a *gorgerin* (mail or

(Below) In heraldry a 'bend' is a diagonal stripe. Many accounts from the time of the Wars of the Rose in England and from various Continental sources mention cloth issued to make 'bends' for soldiers. The quantities issued suggest that a sash-like strip was sometimes worn, presumably from shoulder to hip, over existing liveries. This would be a cheap way to distinguish different commands, e.g. the livery jacket might show the captain's colours, the 'bend' those of an overall commander. In 1450 in the reign of Henry VI we read that 'every Lord whythe hys retenowe' should wear a 'bendys' above his armour so that 'every lorde schulde be knowe from othyr'; and in 1461 every man should wear his lord's livery and 'be-syde alle that, every man and Lorde bare the Pryncys levery', a bend of crimson and black with 'esterygeys' (ostritch) feathers. In 1475 Edward IV paid a long overdue bill for crimson cloth for bends for his knights and squires who fought at Towton in 1461.

Perhaps these bends were sometimes sewn onto the clothes or livery jacket; but we have further evidence for their being worn as sashes. In 1304 the French army campaigning in Flanders were to 'mark themselves with a white *escherpe* (scarf) so that they would be recognised while fighting'. We know that the Armagnacs, enemies of Burgundy, were described as wearing as a distinguishing mark 'a white bend'. In 1445 Philip the Good of Burgundy said that he could not possibly wear the white band (sash) of King Alfonso V's Aragonese Order of the Goblet because it looked too much like the white band adopted by his father's enemies, the Armagnacs. Two portraits of members of the Order, c1440 and 1460, clearly show a white sash-like band of cloth worn diagonally over the left shoulder - which strongly suggests that the Armagnac 'bend' was indeed a sash. (Photo Gerry Embleton; grateful acknowledgement to David Key for use of his research notes)

plate neck protection), with good sleeves, made of 12 layers of cloth, three of them waxed.

Scenes in two different Swiss chronicles show interesting details of the dress of the bodyguard archers. Diebold Schilling (1435-1486) was a soldier who fought at Grandson and Morat in 1476, and who was commissioned to write a three-volume chronicle of those turbulent years. We do not know the identities of the three artists who made the many wonderful drawings, but it seems likely that two had either seen military service or were very keen observers of such things.

In Schilling's first or so-called 'Zurich chronicle' Charles the Bold is shown advancing with his troops, escorted by four archers on foot wearing short puff-sleeved jacks or arming doublets with the red cross of Burgundy on breast and back, sallets and tight hose. Two carry bows and two glaives or spears.

In the 'Berne chronicle' this scene is repeated, the archers wearing the same except for small caps with a single plume and - a detail odd enough to be convincing - their hose rolled up to below the knees (perhaps footless hose rolled up for marching?) All four carry tasselled spears or glaives. These may well be Charles's English archers, who stuck close to him through thick and thin.

A huge number of documents dealing with the Burgundian army survive, but this is by chance. It does not mean that other contemporary armies functioned without the same sort of meticulous accounts and records, nor that other bodyguards and nobles' close retainers were less well equipped, but simply that the documents have not survived - or, as is too frequently the case, survive but have not been analysed and published.

(Opposite) Plate 6:
Livery, 12th to 15th Centuries

(**Above**) This sturdy officer of archers, c1480, wears on his breast the embroidered boar badge of Richard of York and Gloucester, later Richard III of England. (Photo Gerry Embleton)

(**A**) Wall painting, c1170, from the ex-Templer church at Cressac, France, showing the cross badge worn by crusaders. Such illustrations are rare, and when the crusader cross is shown it is usually small. Members of religious orders like this Templer seem to have been the first to adopt it. Later the cross in various forms became the national/military insignia of the major European powers, and was practically a regulation uniform badge by the 15th century.

(**B**) Founded in the 1180s to defend their homes against marauders, the 'White Hoods' of Ghent were reformed in 1379 when their city rose in rebellion against the Count of Flanders.

(**C**) Coloured hoods were a relatively cheap way of showing membership of a guild or allegiance to a town, lord, or political group. Blue and red were the colours of the city of Paris - not always in harmony with its king.

(**D**) In January 1426 the English were resoundingly defeated by the Burgundians at the battle of Brouwershaven. Among the Flemish contingent loyal to Burgundy were the men of the Hague and Delft wearing black and white hoods, and those of Dordrecht wearing red and white.

(**E**) In 1358 kettle hats in the blue and red of Paris were worn by the followers of Etienne Marcel.

(**F**) In 1378 servants and followers of King Charles IV of France and his son, the future Charles V, are depicted wearing half red and half white, or all-red tunics and hose.

(**G**) The infantry of Edward I of England were ordered to wear 'bands' with the red cross of St George during his Welsh wars. Sewn to the soldier's own clothing, jack or brigandine, it became the national badge during the 13th century. Edward III's articles of war ordered it worn; it was displayed by everyone in the Black Prince's army in 1355, and for Richard II's Scottish expedition of 1385. It was increasingly worn on a white jacket by whole English armies, and at times by England's allies. In 1482 the army sent against Scotland were ordered to wear white jackets with the cross of St George front and back and the badges of their captains on the breast.

(**H**) 14th century French forces adopted the white cross as their field sign, the '*vraie enseigne du Roy*'. It was worn on clothing or armour, and frequently on a red or blue jacket or on coloured liveries. In the 15th century the French too wore their captains' badges superimposed.

(**I**) The Burgundians adopted St Andrew's cross as their field sign at the beginning of the 15th century. It was rendered as crossed 'ragged staffs', crossed arrows, or a plain cross, in a variety of colours. By Charles the Bold's accession (1467) it was usually a plain red saltire, worn by his regular 'Ordinance' troops on a blue and white field. By agreement with the King of France the Burgundians were allowed to wear it even when serving with the royal armies.

(**J**) Bretons wore the black cross of St Yves on a white field.

(**K**) Crosses varied in size; they might be sewn onto a jack or brigandine, or onto civilian clothes.

(**L**) For economy, several very simple livery jackets were commonly issued, cut to fit easily over clothes, jacks or armour. This one could be slipped on over the head and belted at the waist. It is in the English national colours, and bears on the left breast the badge of Sir William Tussel, who led a contingent in the 1475 expedition to France. The edges of livery jackets were often bound with contrasting coloured tape.

(**M**) Some manuscripts show groups of uniformly dressed French troops, like this member of an Ordinance company c1470, clothed all in black with livery jackets in their captain's colours and the white cross superimposed. French town contingents sometimes wore uniform colours, or the arms or name of their town embroidered on breast or arm.

(**N**) Another style of jacket - in Breton colours - as worn over armour, cut away at the shoulders and sides so as not to interfere with arm movement.

(**O**) A not uncommon style of jacket with buttoned front, here in the colours of the Earl of Derby and bearing his badge of a yellow eagle's leg, c1475.

(**P**) In the 15th and early 16th centuries Swiss banner bearers, musicians, officers (and in at least one case, *cantinières*) often wore their cantons' colours: here, the blue and white of Lucerne and the red and black of Berne, c1476. They were less worn by common soldiers, who usually came in their own clothes. Sometimes, however, a town would clothe its men alike, such as the contingent of 131 men from St Gallen who were all in red at the battle of Grandson in 1476.

(**Q & R**) Two examples of the heavily embroidered livery jackets which might be worn by household servants and bodyguards, after the Burgundian 'Caesar' tapestry made at Tournai in c1465-70 and presented by Charles the Bold to Guillaume de la Beaume, who served at Grandson and Morat. Decoratively stylised initial letters were often embroidered on breast or sleeves.

(**S**) In the 1460s archers of the bodyguard of Antoine, Bastard of Burgundy, wore red *paletots* bearing his badge of a 'barbican' - the movable wooden cover over a wall embrasure - with a white St Andrew's cross and gold flames. Their hose were green and white.

It is clear that distinctive insignia were a generally accepted way of identifying allies and enemies. There are several recorded examples of confusion arising from similar badges being worn by both sides, and of soldiers passing themselves off by adopting the opponents' insignia. At the siege of Neuss (1475) 600 men from Cologne put on the St Andrew's cross and slipped through the Burgundian siege lines into the town each carrying 40lbs of gunpowder.

A B C D E F

G H I J K

L M N O P

Q R S

(Opposite) Plate 7:
15th Century Livery and Badges

(A) Reconstruction of the arming coat of Charles, Duke of Burgundy, showing the heraldic arms of his possessions. Costly embroidery, rich fabrics, gold and silver wire and pearls were often worn over their armour by the mighty. A fortune was lavished on all those who accompanied them to war - ministers, councillors, servants, bodyguards, heralds and trumpeters - a kaleidoscope of colours, heraldic devices and decorative fantasy.

(B) Tentative reconstruction - from a description in the memoirs of Jean de Haynin - of the *paletot* worn by the bodyguards of Charles, Count of Charolais, later Duke of Burgundy, during the 1465 campaign. This attempts to illustrate the richness of decoration frequently displayed by troops of this class.

(C) The bodyguard archers of Louis de Luxembourg, Constable of France and an ally of Burgundy.

(D) The followers of Louis de Bruges, Seigneur de la Gruuthuuse c1466, may have worn his colours of violet and white with the red saltire of Burgundy or his bombard badge.

(E) The followers of the Seigneur de Hames.

(F) Jean de Luxembourg's archers in the 1465 Monthlery campaign.

Documentary evidence allows the reconstruction of the liveries of several other Burgundian nobles: Seigneur d'Esquerdes, white and green, red saltire; Jean de Rubempré, Grand Bailly de Hainault 1466, black and violet, white saltire; Antoine Rolin, Seigneur d'Aymeries 1466, white and blue, red saltire; Hugh de Neuville, Sénéchal de Saint Pol (who commanded the advance guard at Monthlery), red, perhaps without the cross of Burgundy.

(G to L) Some of the many English liveries worn during the Wars of the Roses:

(G) Sir John Wogan, with his badge of a 'cockentrice' - a beast half cockerel, half dragon. His motto was '*garde vous*' - 'be careful' or 'look out'.

(H) The blue and 'murray' livery of King Edward IV of England bears one version of his 'sun in splendour' badge combined with the white rose of York.

(I) Richard Neville, Earl of Warwick and Salisbury, whose men also wore a standing bear and ragged staff badge, c1458.

(J) Henry Stafford, Duke of Buckingham.

(K) Lord Ferrers. Like many nobles of his day he is known to have used several badges - this gold horseshoe, a white greyhound running, a gold crown, and a 'French wife's hood'.

(L) In 1475 the followers of Thomas Howard, Duke of Norfolk wore his red and white livery jacket with a white sallet badge. On the Scottish expedition one of his men, Robert Coke, had 'a peirre brigandines, a standard (i.e. a mail collar), a salate (sallet), a chef (sheaf) of arowes, a peir of splentys (splints - probably chain and plate arm protection) and his jaket, a gusset (probably mail shorts)'.

(M) Embroidered badge which seems to have been used by Charles the Bold's bodyguard archers in the 1470s, and was painted on their banners captured at Grandson in 1476.

(N) Metal badges were issued to retainers at all levels, in silver or gold for those nearest the great princes - bodyguards and servants in the royal households - and in cheap pewter or lead to tens of thousands of the more humble. This badge excavated in London combines the Plantagenet 'sunburst' emblem with the traditional rose of Edward IV.

(O) Pewter badge of the Duke of Warwick's 'ragged staff' emblem - also one of René of Anjou's badges.

(P) Many late 15th century chronicle illustrations show the Swiss wearing their white cross badge in these various positions - but not all at once… The commonest are on breast, sleeve or thigh; they rarely appear on the helmet or hood.

(Q) 'Bends' or diagonal sashes may have been a fairly common way to distinguish groups of troops within an overall command - see page 47. (A band - a strip of cloth or colour - origin 'bende'. Old French, 15th century, a word of Germanic origin. *Collins New English Dictionary*)

(R) A coloured hood, a breast badge, and an embroidered initial or slogan on the sleeve - three common ways of distinguishing different commands, though not necessarily worn together.

(S) The badge of Charles, Duke of Bourbon 1434-56 - a fire pot or 'feu grégois' (Greek fire).

(T) One of René of Anjou's possessions was Lorraine, referred to by one of his badges, this double-barred cross and crown.

(U) In an age without 'mass media' to establish their prestige, and thus to some extent their security, rulers depended on so impressing eyewitnesses that tales of their power and glory would spread by word of mouth - and grow in the telling. They spent fortunes on display - great pageants, tournaments, and triumphal entries into conquered or submitted towns. Louis XII of France (1498-1515) wore this amazing ensemble for his ceremonial entry into a captured city during his Italian campaign. It is embroidered with one of his personal badges, bees and hives, and a motto - '*non vtitura cv leores*' ?

(V) The gentlemen of his bodyguard wore coats of various colours bearing another of his badges, a crown and porcupine richly embroidered in gold.

(**Above**) A splendid officer of Italian militia, with a plumed turban on his sallet and the boar badge of his town on his jack. (Photo John Howe)

A

B

C

D

E

F

G

H

I

J

K

L

M

N

O

P

Q

R

S

T

U

V

(**Left**) This French artillery or engineer officer wears simple, practical clothes and ankle boots, with the national livery displayed. He covers his outfit with a sumptuous gown of red and gold Italian cloth trimmed with dark fur. He is a man of great wealth, completely absorbed in a new passion, and can well afford to use such an expensive gown as the equivalent of a mechanic's overalls. On his head he wears his hood rolled into a hat, a practical no-nonsense headgear.

In the 15th century the term 'artillery' did not mean simply the cannons and their impedimenta, but also what we might call the 'logistic' branch of an army. We know from surviving accounts that the 'artillery' looked after all sorts of supplies including transport, bows, crossbows, ammunition, tentage, bridge-building and camp equipment. They meticulously record the purchase and cost of everything from archers' gloves and linen cord for crossbow strings to pigs of lead for shot and paint for gun carriages.

Some 20th century historians have underestimated the efficiency of 15th century gunnery. There is ample evidence that pre-weighed and wrapped powder charges - in Napoleonic terms, 'fixed cartridge' - and multiple detachable breech chambers made light breech-loading field guns entirely practical (see page 54). Siege artillery - the heavy bombards which were dug and wedged into static positions after being transported across country with immense labour - was a hugely expensive investment, in which no prince would have indulged without a practical return in terms of multiplication of force. Guns made a real difference. For instance, the Neopolitan castle of Monte San Giovanni had in the past withstood a siege for seven years. In 1494 it fell to the guns of Charles VIII's army in eight hours. (Photo John Howe)

Masters of Artillery

An important development during the 15th century was the huge increase in the use of artillery, both light field pieces and immensely powerful bombards for siege work. The complex equipment and huge wagon trains needed to support these new weapons led to the emergence of a new class of craftsman officer, and of companies of engineers, metalworkers, powder and shot makers, sappers and wagoners - whose high cost ate up a considerable part of the available military budgets. New developments were led by France and Burgundy. Those noblemen with an intense interest in mechanics and science could follow a new career as 'masters of artillery'.

(Above & right) In hot weather and for hard labour the doublet might be thrown back and left hanging behind, still fastened at the waist by the bottom front buttons and still supporting the laced-on hose, which were not made high enough at the waist to be self-supporting until the end of the 15th century. The sleeves are sometimes shown tied together at the front. Sleeveless 'doublets', cut like a modern waistcoat, did not appear until the very end of the century. The only written mention of them in a military context is in Louis XI of France's orders for a type of jack to be worn by his troops, without a shirt but over a sleeveless skeleton doublet of linen to support the hose.

All the craftsmen vital to an army's functioning had to be recruited and paid. In 1456 Philip the Good of Burgundy dreamed of a crusade against the Turks, and put detailed plans on paper. These involved some 500 to 600 carpenters, bowyers, fletchers, crossbow makers, gunners, masons, smiths, miners, pioneers and workmen, all to be armed with pikes or 'defensive weapons', ready to fight under the command of the master of artillery, ' … and to be paid archer's wages of 3 petards a day'. This shows clearly that all these artisans were considered the equals of well-paid professional infantry, and were not poor peasants dressed in rags.

We can be sure that any medieval army on campaign needed a similar workforce, but we do not know if it was dressed from one source, wore the livery of different captains or those of the towns they came from. We know that in the mid-century Burgundian pioneers were all ordered to wear jacks with the Burgundian cross; and we can be sure that those craftsmen used to wearing an apron for their work would have continued to do so. (Photos John Howe)

(**Left**) The interest in the science and mechanics of siegecraft made the engineer and gunner men of great importance. Several famous artists served in such roles, including Leonardo da Vinci and Michaelangelo, who boasted of his mastery of the science of fortification. This is a reconstruction of a 15th century book with fold-out parchment pages illustrating the mechanics of artillery and sieges. Such manuals seem to have held great interest for the medieval military. Careful examination of the many which survive - some unpublished - reveals a level of sophistication that is difficult to absorb. Attempts to recreate some of their depicted siege equipment and gun carriages have quickly converted scepticism to delighted astonishment: while the relative scales shown may be odd, the essentials of design have been found to be entirely sound.

(**Right**) The Company of St George, which represents an artillery company of the Burgundian wars c1476, has experimented for several years with its two carefully constructed breech-loading 'field guns'. Prolonged practical trials have proved these quarter-ton weapons to be highly manoeuvrable, and both accurate and long-ranged with stone and iron shot (e.g. one gun achieved a three-shot group just over one metre across, and a virtually flat trajectory, on a Swiss army 300-metre range). Contemporary illustrations show several separate breeches laid ready by these guns; with three breeches each and six-strong crews, the reconstructed cannon have proved capable of safely laying down an extremely rapid barrage of fire. (Photos John Howe)

Music and Games

From king to peasant the ability to sing, play a musical instrument and dance were so much appreciated as to be considered normal accomplishments. Soldiers could entertain themselves just as they did at home (and had far more leisure with the army than they ever did in their own villages). The small pipe and drum, flute, fife and bagpipe which were played at village celebrations naturally became the instruments for the march; presumably the players improvised on popular folk melodies, nearly all now sadly lost to us. Swiss troops in the 15th century are frequently shown marching behind musicians, who are sometimes dressed in the livery of their canton; armoured soldiers are shown dancing hand in hand. Trumpeters and drummers sent signals in camp, on the march and in battle, and played for celebrations.

Minstrels - a term covering a multitude of entertainers from acrobats, jokers, dancers, and jugglers to fine musicians, and many who could do all of these things - formed part of the retinue of nobleman and king. Many were also messengers, clerks, companions, even spies and soldiers, and some won fame and honour. The Black Prince took four French pipers on his 'great raid' in 1355; since he bought for them not only 'rayed' (striped) cloth for robes but also two mail shirts, and a kettle hat for 'Jakelyn Piper', we may assume that more than music was expected of them.

Story-telling was a great pastime at every level, and clowning, grotesque jokes and bawdiness were much enjoyed. Many of what are now considered children's games, played with much crude and violent humour, were widely popular, as were skittles, dice, cards, nine man's morris, and sports such as wrestling, races and football (Photos: left, David Lazenby, Middelaldercentret; below, Gerry Embleton).

Francs Archiers

(Above & above right) A 'free archer' wearing a French livery jacket (note the capped shoulders) over parti-coloured red and white doublet and hose.

The longbow was not an entirely English weapon. There were many excellent archers in Flanders, Germany and France, some serving in 'English' companies. Nor was the bow always the weapon of yeomen or commoners alone. An ordinance of 1425 issued by Jean, fifth Duke of Brittany, ordered that '… nobles of less estate are to furnish themselves with the habiliments of archers in brigandines, if they know how to use the bow, otherwise they are to be furnished with good *guisarmes* and good *salades* and leg harness and have each a *coustilleur* and two good horses. Nobles of still less retinue are to wear brigandines and good salades, or at least good *paletock*, armed in the new fashion without sleeves, with overlapping plates of iron or mail on their arms, with good guisarmes or bows, if

they know how to use them'.

In an unsuccessful attempt to raise a force equivalent to the powerful bowmen of England Charles VII of France, in 1448, ordained that each parish in his kingdom should equip an archer 'with huque of brigandine or jack, salade, sword, dagger, bow, quiver or crossbow' (furnished with its accessories). These soldiers were declared exempt from all taxes. They wore the white national cross, and sometimes the livery of the village or captain.

We have a drawing of a lost effigy of Guillaume le May, a captain of these *francs archiers* who died in 1480. He wears a brigandine with short sleeves also of brigandine work which appear to be tied on, leg and arm harness, a dagged skirt and collar of mail. His livery jacket bears the French cross and is cut away at the sides of the body to allow free movement of the arms. His bow looks exactly like a typical English weapon.

(Below) These arrows show typical construction details - the feathers (fletchings) are glued and tied to the shaft with linen thread. The nocks (slots for the bowstring to rest in) are reinforced with a sliver of horn set into the shaft. The single coloured fletching of the three instantly indicates to the archer which should face away from the bow when the arrow was nocked, so that the two uncoloured fletchings lay flat against the stave. (Photos John Howe)

15th Century English Soldiers

(Above) By the mid-15th century there were many gentlemen, not knights, who were rich enough to own full armour. Different qualities were available at prices to suit all purses. In most battles only a part of these 'men-at-arms' and their lords now fought on horseback as the shock or tactical reserve element; many fought on foot, forming the front ranks of the blocks of soldiers, and usually wielding pole-axes and other long weapons. Here armoured English soldiers of the Wars of the Roses gather around their banner, drummer and commander to receive instructions. They wear an interesting mixture of armour, some under livery jackets. The two in the right foreground, fully armoured except for their booted lower legs, are horsemen who have dismounted to fight.

(Right) This mid-15th century archer wears the livery badge of his master, the Earl of Stafford, on his red coat. This is a well-

paid man able to afford rich ornaments for belt, sword and purse, and no doubt a coat of fine mail under his jacket.

The three great victories over the French - Crécy (1345), Poitiers (1356) and Agincourt (1415) - made the English archer a legend. Though much about him remains obscure, occasional surviving descriptions give us a glimpse of him. We know the names of some who fought at Agincourt: David Cock, John Grafton, Lewis Hunte, Richard Whityngton (was he Dick to his friends?), William Jauderal, Yanthlos. We have a description of what they mostly wore:
' … without armour to their pourpoints, their hosen loosened, having hatchets and axes, long swords hanging from their girdles and some with their feet naked: some wore *humettes* or caps of *cuir bouilli* or wicker work crossed over with iron' (St Remy). (Photos Gerry Embleton)

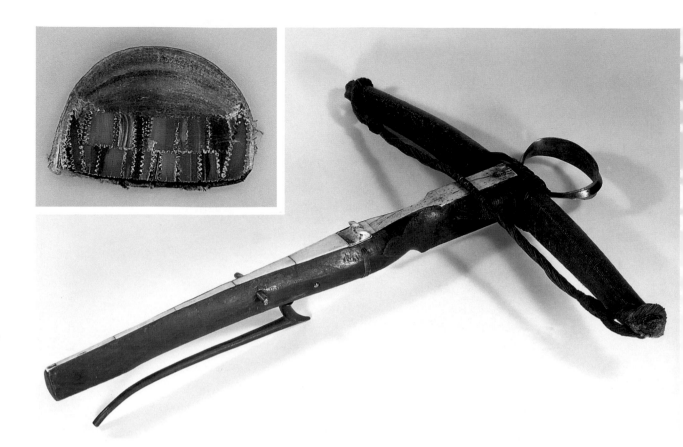

(Above) A wonderful original example of a composite crossbow, Swiss, c1470s. We have lost the skills to make these bows today, and surviving examples are too precious for us to test their shooting capabilities, but they were certainly powerful. All nations used both longbows and crossbows, but in Germany, Switzerland and northern Italy a tradition of crossbow marksmanship grew up, accompanied by the sort of tall tales and legendary characters which surrounded the longbow in England. Light bows were used for hunting, and very large ones, bent for loading by means of levers, were common in castle defence.(Photo Ian Ashdown)

(Inset above) A fascinating insight into lost medieval skills, this cross section of a composite crossbow stave shows that the inside or 'belly' (here, at the bottom) was assembled from irregular pieces of horn - in the photo back-lighting makes them glow orange. They were meticulously grooved to make tight joints and then glued together; we do not know what adhesive was used, but the method was clearly so effective that the final composite structure was symmetrical, balanced, and could take the massive strain of repeated bending and releasing. The (upper) 'back' of the stave was made from sinew, the outer covering from parchment, birch bark, or - as here - heavy paper with a densely printed pattern. (Photo Gerry Embleton)

(Left) An English crossbowman in Yorkist service during the Wars of the Roses. He wears a breastplate over a padded, short-sleeved jack in the colours of King Edward IV of England. His clothes and equipment are of good quality but show signs of hard campaigning. His powerful steel bow needs a cranequin to load it (see also page 74). (Photo Gerry Embleton)

(Right) These typical English archers show two different styles of national livery jackets over a mixture of padded jacks and mail. Both wear light helmets, one what we call today an 'archer's sallet', the other a visored sallet. Dominic Mancini described the troops of the Dukes of Gloucester and Buckingham summoned to London in 1485:

'There is hardly any without a helmet, and none without bows and arrows. Their bows and arrows are thicker and longer than those used by other nations, just as their bodies are stronger than other peoples; for they seem to have hands and arms of iron. The range of their bow is no less than our arbalests (crossbows); there hangs by the side of each a sword no less long than ours, but heavy and thick as well. The sword is always accompanied by an iron shield … They do not wear any metal armour on their breast or any other part of their body, except for the better sort … '
(Photo Alan & Michael Perry)

(Left) During lulls in the Hundred Years War and after its close in the 1450s, the French countryside swarmed with unemployed soldiers. These two wear good stout travelling clothes, and still have some of their last pay left. The only trade they know is soldiering; they are experienced and dangerous men, looking for someone to serve. Their weapons are well cared for. Note the crossbowman's cranequin, and the fist buckler - Mancini's 'iron shield' - hanging from his sword hilt.

They travel through territories bedevilled by bands of their former comrades and enemies, more or less desperate, fighting each other and the peasants and preying mercilessly on anyone weaker than themselves. In England the situation was slightly less out of control, but many ex-soldiers became outlaws - 'Wastoures, Roberdsmen and Drawlatches'. There were labouring jobs to be found, and many took to the roads. In a society that viewed the homeless with suspicion, to cross the line from employed soldier to beggar and vagabond was to become an enemy of society. Any suspicion of wrongdoing and the stocks and prison were waiting. And let us not underestimate what imprisonment could mean in those days:

In the reign of Henry III 'two men, aliens and a woman' were imprisoned at Thorleston and detained without charges, until one died and 'the other lost one foot, the woman lost either foot by putrefaction'- presumably from the fetters. When finally taken for trial the court was 'loth to try them, because they were not attached for any robbery or misdeed', and let them depart. How they departed, and whither, remains unrecorded.
(Photo Gerry Embleton)

15th Century German Soldiers

In the 1460s-70s many German and Swiss small cities and towns employed mercenaries or small bands of their own townspeople as security forces. In such troubled times many citizens preferred to pay for substitutes rather than serve themselves. Swordsmen like this soldier, trained in fighting with the hand-and-a-half sword and practised during many inter-city squabbles, were sought-after professionals. In war he would also carry a halberd. Germany and Switzerland did not then exist as separate political nations; a soldier's loyalty would be firstly to whoever paid him, and secondly to the Emperor and those who spoke his language.

He wears good quality clothes and a fine sallet, breast and back plates and gauntlets, in the ribbed and pointed style much favoured by what might be called the 'common soldier' of the German-speaking world. His armour is

well-fitted, cleverly hammered to shape to reduce the weight to a necessary minimum while keeping the most vulnerable points thick enough to withstand blows. His sallet skull is hammered out of one piece of metal, its compound curves graceful and subtle. Even the most workaday 'ammunition armour' retained these qualities.

Armour was transported wrapped in blanket material, packed in straw in barrels, or in baskets (though the *Chronique de Troyes* of the 1470s mentions that French troops were specifically forbidden to carry theirs in *paniers*). On campaign it needed constant maintenance. Broken straps and buckles and the rivets holding the different plates together had to be replaced or repaired; a broken shoulder strap at an awkward moment could make an armour unwearable. (Photos Anne Embleton)

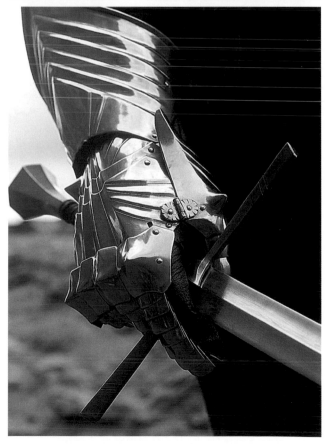

(**Top left**) The most common protection for the neck was a mail collar ('standard'), usually lined, fastened with buckles, buttons or hooks at side or back, like this example. (Photo Gerry Embleton)

(**Centre left**) All men and women had small possessions to carry - money, keys, an eating knife, perhaps a spoon, a handkerchief ('muckinder'), a comb, etc. They carried them in a purse firmly fixed to their belt. A knife or dagger frequently hung behind the purse, out of the way. Only very rarely were cups and other items hung from the belt, and contemporary pictures of soldiers almost never show even a purse. Anything dangling from a waist belt could be too easily lost or stolen; no doubt such things were carried under the coat or jacket. Women frequently wore their purses hanging between their shirts and their skirts. Metal ornaments were popular, their weight helping to keep the flap of the purse down - in crudely cast lead, in pewter or brass for the humbler sort, in silver and gilt for the wealthy.

An early 16th century book lists what a servant should have ready for his master to carry when travelling - and it might equally apply to a well-paid 15th century household archer: 'Purse, dagger, cloak, night cap, kerchief, shoeing horn, wallet, shoes, spear, bag, hood, halter, saddle cloth, spurs, hat, horse comb, bow, arrows, sword, buckler, gloves, string, bracer, pen, paper, ink, parchment, red wax, pumice (eraser), books, penknife, comb, thimble, needle, thread, spare points, bodkin, knife, shoemaker's thread'. (Photo Anne Embleton)

(**Bottom left**) These stout ankle boots have hobnails, 'clump' soles (two layers, sewn together internally), and are closed with two buckles and a point. (Photo Anne Embleton)

(**Above**) Deep kettle hats with or without eye slits and aventails were popular in the German-speaking Empire and Bohemia. (Photo Gerry Embleton)

(Right) Officer of the Black Forest infantry contingent in the 1474 campaign, dressed in black and armed with pole-axe and sword. Note the slit sleeves of his hooded overgown.

Many town contingents were properly equipped and uniformed expeditionary forces. To give some picture of the 15th century army on the march and in camp, we cite one example among many. In 1431 Regensburg sent its contribution to the army going against the invading Hussites. Following the commander marched 73 horsemen and 71 crossbowmen with the banner. Next 16 handgunners preceded a wagon with a crucifix and a chaplain. Supporting personnel included smiths, leather workers, pike makers and armourers, tailors, cooks and butchers. There were six cannon with shot and lead; 41 wagons loaded with powder and more lead, 60,000 crossbow bolts and arrows, 300 fire arrows, 19 handguns, cowhides for the stables and tents, and corn for six weeks. Provisions included cooked meat and bacon, 1,200 cheeses, 80 stockfish, candles, vinegar, olive oil, saffron, ginger, Austrian wine and a vast supply of beer. Ninety oxen followed with their herders.

We have references to many uniformed contingents - e.g. Frankfurt in red and white, Nuremberg all in red. Strasbourg levies wore half-red, half-white tunics from the 14th century, as did the contingents raised by its guilds and the mercenaries paid by the city. In 1473 Augsburg wore red, white and green. In 1474 Walshut and the Black Forest soldiers were all in black, Colmar in red and blue. That year Johan von Venningen, Bishop of Basel, mobilised 1,000 men in red tunics with the colours of the bishopric on their left arms. In 1459 the Count Palatine of the Rhine sent 1,300 men to aid the Landgrave of Hesse all clothed in his blue and white. We also read of wagons uniformly painted, each with a recognition sign.

(Below) Light armour, like this worn by two German swordsmen at practice c1470, was also popular for war. Many soldiers seem to have gone without leg protection for the sake of mobility.
(Photos Gerry Embleton)

(Opposite) Plate 8: Gambesons, Jacks and Brigandines

Jack, pourpoint, heuk, brigandine, haubergeon, gambeson, hacketon and *arming coat* were terms used freely by medieval writers to describe a range of garments, mostly defensive. Different words are sometimes used in the same document to describe the same thing; at other times the same words refer to different things, whose distinctions were obviously clear to the writer - though not to us. Today we generally refer to padded fabric defences as jacks - although we also read of 'jakkes stufyd (lined) with horn' and of 'black lynen stuffyd with mail'. Those consisting of small plates riveted between layers of cloth are termed brigandines. Pourpoints, arming doublets and arming coats might be jackets displaying heraldic charges, or padded protective or foundation garments worn beneath armour or to support the hose. Wealthy men sometimes combined such protection with fine fabrics, embroidery, jewels and fur.

In 1444 we read of 'a pourpoint of leather with 6 layers of cloth'; and of another of black fustian with sleeves, to wear under armour. Sir John Paston wrote home on 3 June 1473 for 'a new vestment of wyght damaske for a dekyn (deacon) which is among myn other geer at Norwich. I will make an armying doublet of it.'

(Below) Among Burgundian troops besieging Velexon castle in 1409-10 were 30 'armed men' and 15 crossbowmen sent from Dijon for one month's service, 'dressed and ready to go'. Vermilion cloth was supplied 'from which were cut the letters Dijon put on the sleeve of each jack', backed with white cloth 'in the form of a scroll'. There are many other examples of lettering being used as badges. In 1464 a contingent sent north from Nottingham were issued with red 'jakettes and a yard of white fustian was used to cut out letters and set them on the jackettes'. (Photos Gerry Embleton)

(A) The footsoldier's padded gambeson shown in the Maciejowski Bible, c1250, changed little over 250 years. Men's lives depended on how evenly such garments were padded and how little they restricted movement. Making them was skilled work, and strict regulations attempted to control their quality. Among many examples, regulations from Paris in 1296 laid down the required materials and construction. In 1322 Edward II ordered the Armourers' Company of London to ensure that 'Akton and Gabezon' were made of good quality materials, and that 'ye wyite acketonnes be stuffed of old (soft) lynnen and of cottone and of new cloth wyth in and wyth out'.

(B) 15th century writers mention the characteristic thigh-length 'soft' jacks of English troops. In 1483 the Duke of Gloucester's men were described as wearing jacks 'stuffed with tow … The softer the tunics the better do they withstand the blows of arrows and swords'. Fouquet portrayed footsoldiers in long padded garments, sometimes worn under mail shirts, presenting a similar silhouette. The later Flemish artist Memling shows close-fitting, fashionably-waisted jacks.

(C) A breastplate, or simply the lower half (a *plackart*) fitted comfortably on the stiff, tailored jack. *Braies d'acier* - mail shorts tied to a doublet - were often worn beneath. (Memling, Reliquary of St Ursula, c1489)

(D) Jack worn under mail shoulder pieces but over a mail skirt or *braies d'acier*. (Memling, The Passion, c1480s)

(E) Beautiful rendering of a well-fitted jack. Tied to the arms are chain-like metal defences which may perhaps be the 'splints' often mentioned in contemporary documents. (Memling, Reliquary of St Ursula, c1489)

(F) Note the flared skirt and deep cut-outs to give maximum freedom of movement. Thick, protective shoulder fringes of cord or leather appear in several 15th century sources. (Memling, The Passion, c1480s)

(G) Another example of tied-on defences made of bars, rings and small plates. (Burgundian tapestry, Siege of Jerusalem by Titus, c1460)

(H & I) The Schilling Chronicles often show short jacks with high collars and short, padded sleeves worn by archers, probably English, in Burgundian service. Their very thick bows, small helmets, large arrow bags and high collars are exaggerated, as if the artist had seen these distinctive features.

(J) Typical late 15th century velvet-covered brigandine. The nails are tinned against rust and set in threes. The edges of the plates forming the right side are left uncovered so that they slide easily under the left side and are overlapped when the brigandine is buckled. It is rigid enough to stand up by itself, but flexible enough to be put on like a jacket.

(K) The same construction was used for more complex defences with short sleeves, flared skirts and tassets. This example is worn over plate arm defences, tied to an arming doublet of which the collar is visible. The hose with points will support thigh-length boots, a typical 'half-armed' dress when on campaign.

(L) Many rigid, cloth-covered defences are illustrated; they are studded with fewer rivets than the brigandines often shown alongside them, suggesting fewer, larger plates.

(M) Attached shoulder defences are not uncommon. (French MS, c1450-1470)

(N) These shoulder pieces may be part of a full brigandine worn beneath a livery jacket and over plate arm defences. (Fouquet, Heures d'Etienne Chevalier)

(O) Construction of a brigandine, showing how the slightly curved, overlapping plates were riveted to the fabric jacket.

(P) Towards the end of the 15th century brigandines made of many small plates showing large numbers of rivets became fashionable, like this Italian example. It has tasset extensions tied to the skirt, and is worn over a mail shirt with three-quarter sleeves. (Carpaccio, Arrival of St Ursula in Cologne, c1490)

Jacks and Brigandines

(**Above & above right**) A well armed Burgundian foot soldier wearing a padded jack under a breastplate in 'German' style.

The secret of the jack's success was its layers of soft linen, held in place with rows of stitching and tailored so as not to restrict movement. There are many references to jacks in 15th century accounts, Burgundian, French and English. Careful reconstructions prove that cunning tailoring and variations in the thickness of the padding make jacks remarkably comfortable and allow freedom of movement combined with good protection. The shoulders of the jack are extremely well padded against blows, and the 18 layers of linen - reduced at the waist - give ample protection on their own even without the breast plate, which sits snug and immobile on the tailored body.

It must be emphasised that the jack is not made like a modern 'duvet' or Continental quilt, with two thicknesses sewn into tubular compartments which are then filled with stuffing. Obviously a blade would pass easily through the stitched but unpadded areas. When making a jack the needle and thread must pass right through all the layers of linen or thick padding so that there are no weak spots. (Photos John Howe)

(**Right**) The evening sun emphasises some of the complex tailoring of this severely cut example seen from the back. (Photo Gerry Embleton)

(**Opposite**) Our footsoldier is armed with a beautiful hand-and-a-half sword, with a system of straps that can be worn as a waist belt or over the shoulder. Note the small knife and sharpening steel let into the upper face of the scabbard. (Photo John Howe)

(**Left**) This jack is made with 18 layers of linen. Louis XI of France's ordinance of c1470 is the best surviving description of their construction:

'And first they must have for the said jacks, thirty, or at least twenty-five, folds of cloth, and a stag's skin; those of thirty, with the stag's skin, being the best cloth that has been worn and rendered flexible, is best for this purpose, and these jacks should be made in four quarters. The sleeves should be as strong as the body, with the exception of the leather, and the arm-hole (*assiette*) of the sleeve must be large, which arm-hole should be placed near the collar, not on the bone of the shoulder, that it may be broad under the arm-pit and full under the arm, sufficiently ample and large on the sides below. The collar should be like the rest of the jack, but not made too high behind, to allow room for the salade. This jack should be laced in front, and under the opening must be a hanging piece (*porte piece*) of the same strength as the jack itself. Thus the jack will be secure and easy, provided there be a pourpoint without sleeves or collar of two folds of cloth, that shall be only four fingers broad on the shoulder; to which pourpoint shall be attached the hose. Thus shall the wearer float, as it were, within his jack, and be at his ease; for never have been seen half-a-dozen men killed by stabs or arrow wounds in such jacks, particularly if they be troops accustomed to fighting.'

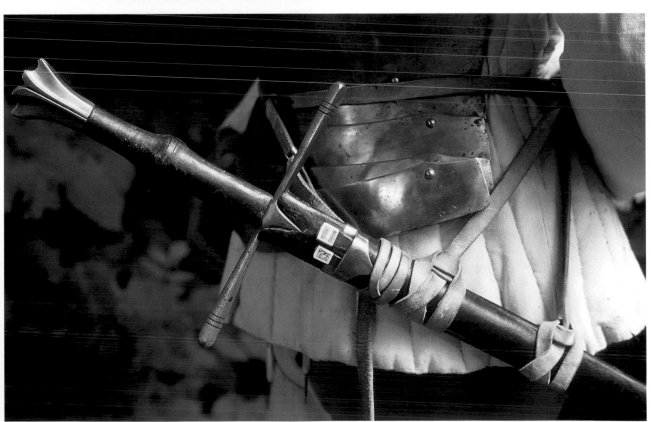

Brigandines were produced in their thousands in various qualities: strong and simple, with a minimum of plates and covered in cheap fustian, or in rich fabric with gilded nails. In the 1460s one of the archer guard of the Duke of Berry wore 'a black velvet covered brigandine with gilt nails, bearing a white cross and on his head a *bicoquet*' (perhaps a contemporary name for a sallet). We know that old armour was sometimes cut up to make brigandine plates. There is some evidence that large parts of obsolete breastplates may have been used - an obvious and practical source for the two large so-called 'lung plates' which formed the chest of some brigandines, and perhaps also for the infinite variety of fabric-covered defences found in illustrations which have fewer and more widely spaced rivets holding them together, indicating larger plates.

(**Above & right**) This French soldier wears a simple brigandine, a light and serviceable protection for the coming assault. It has rivets set singly rather than decoratively in threes, and buckles down the front. Usually brigandines were fastened at side and shoulder with buckled straps, but some had front openings, and one at least has points and eyelets reinforced with metal rings. While his comrades, wearing French livery, begin to assault the defended farm they must capture, he buckles the chin strap of his helmet (and multiplies the protective qualities of his brigandine with a rosary and a prayer …)

Several 15th century brigandines survive. One in Paris is covered with leather, but velvet and fustian (a textile of mixed cotton and flax) seem to be the usual coverings; certainly some kind of tough, densely woven cloth is needed to hold the rivets. (Photos John Howe)

Handgunners

This handgunner is a member of the garrison of the small and rather dilapidated castle of Vaumarcus in what is now Switzerland. In late February 1476 he is scouting the hills above the castle, wrapped in his winter cloak. From the south he can hear the slow thud of guns from Grandson, where the mighty Burgundian army of Charles the Bold is attacking the lakeside castle held by a Bernese garrison. It is an ominous reminder that the greatest army in the world is advancing just a few miles away; and it is as well for our handgunner that he does not yet know the fate that awaits the Bernese when the castle falls.

The lands of Rudolf von Hochberg, Count of Neuchâtel, lie on the borders of territory seized by aggressive Berne on one side and the Burgundian empire on the other. He has tried to stay neutral, but peace talks between the belligerents in 1475 brought little more than a month-long truce. Now the Swiss Confederate army is moving to the relief of Grandson, and the Burgundians are advancing on Rudolf's castle at Vaumarcus, which is caught neatly between the crab's claws.

The commander has been told to surrender as quickly as possible if attacked, but it is a very dangerous situation. Who can imagine that the Confederates have a chance of beating the mighty duke? - yet the Bernese Bear is a powerful and ruthless enemy. In a tiny castle like Vaumarcus it is impossible to keep secrets, and all the occupants share their captain's anxiety: which way to jump?

In fact Vaumarcus surrendered to the Burgundians; but when the Confederates arrived in Neuchâtel the count's military forces joined them. A few days later, on 2 March 1476, they won an extraordinary victory over the Burgundians at the battle of Grandson.

The Bernese then burned Vaumarcus - after stripping it of everything down to the very window-frames - in punishment for having surrendered to Charles too easily … (Photo John Howe)

(Opposite) Period illustrations of 'foul weather gear' are not particularly common, but most show cloaks. Worn by all classes for travelling, riding, or about town in rain or snow, they would have been the commonest cold weather garment for soldiers. Short cloaks were fashionable and practical for riding. A full cloak of good woollen cloth, cut as more than two-thirds of a circle of material, can be wrapped round the body to give excellent warmth and protection. If tightly woven from wool with most of the oil left in, it repels water very well. Cloaks were fastened on the breast with cords, points, or - most often - with two or three pairs of buttons, strongly sewn in place as they take the full strain of the cloak's weight. The rear view illustrates the ample folds, and the long tail (liripipe) of his hood - rather old-fashioned by the 1470s. A full-cut cloak also made practical bedding, with enough material to serve as both 'mattress and blanket'. This was all the shelter that many a medieval soldier knew when on campaign. (Photos John Howe)

(Right) This handgunner wears a simple but thick woollen gown, less cumbersome than a cloak. The ample sleeves are slit to allow his hands to pass through when shooting or working. Burgundian livery is visible beneath. (Photo Philippe Krauer, *l'Illustré*)

(Below) Late 15th century handgunners display their weapons. The left hand man gun has the smouldering match held at the top of a simple external S-shaped lever, sprung to drop forwards when the lower half is pulled back. The more advanced gun on the right has trigger and serpentine (match holder) made separately; the lever action of the trigger being lifted drops the match into the priming pan. (Photo Gerry Embleton)

(Above & left) Most mid-15th century armies included increasing numbers of handgunners. Burgundian gunners are depicted in manuscripts as lightly armoured, and holding their guns both on top of the shoulder and pulled into it like modern firearms. The third quarter of the century saw development of the 'matchlock', with a trigger, a spring- or button-released serpentine holding the match, a swivelling pan cover and a ramrod held in place below the barrel.

(Right) Gunners carried powder in a metal flask, gourd or horn; a bag for bullets, match, and perhaps a bullet mould, since guns were not made with standard bores. One late 15th century drawing in the Schilling Chronicles shows handgunners in action, and lying close by a two-compartment ammunition box with balls in one section and prepared charges - cartridges - in the other. (Photos John Howe)

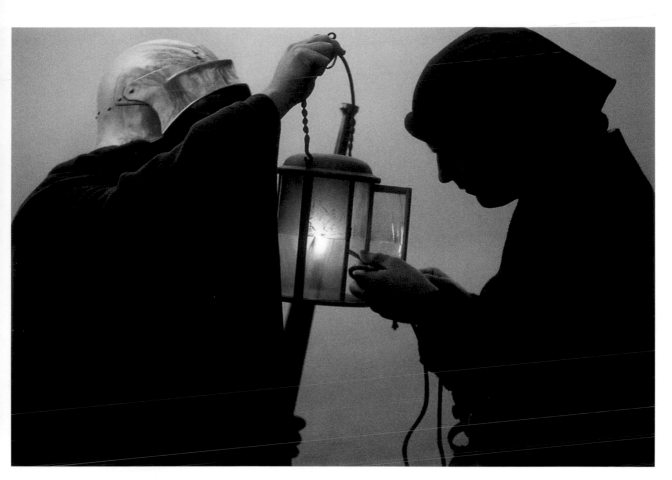

(Above) Soldiers and townsfolk spent a lot of time on guard duty, day and night, making their rounds in camp or on the walls with lanterns and passwords. In bad weather they wrapped up in heavy gowns, cloaks and hoods, some issued specifically for 'watching'. Here our Neuchâtel handgunner relights his slowmatch from a lantern on the ramparts of Vaumarcus. (Photo John Howe)

(Left) A Burgundian handgunner with a felt hat and no armour. Tired, unshaven and dirty, he has been skirmishing in the woods near Morat against Swiss scouts in late May 1476. The duke's ordinances strictly regulated the arms and armour of his troops, but how far they were followed in the three months between the ruinous losses at Grandson and the reorganisation of the army to attack Morat is difficult to say. (Photo John Howe)

Careful working reconstructions reveal the late 15th century handgun to be a handy enough (if very short-range) weapon, more efficient than is often imagined. Again, we must accept the verdict of the day: if it had not been useful they would not have carried it. In fact the Swiss and Germans organised mixed units of handgun and crossbow skirmishers in a sort of 'light infantry' called *Schützenfähnlein,* with banners bearing images of bow and gun. We must assume that handguns had some relative tactical value - beyond the obvious one: that a boy like this could now crook his finger and send to his tomb a prince of the blood wearing and riding a fortune.

> We are alike both outward and within,
> Our hunger is satisfied with the same fare,
> And when our bones into confusion fall,
> Say, who know the living man by sight,
> Which is the villein now and which the knight?
>
> *Walther von der Vogelweide*

15th Century Swiss Soldiers

(**Above**) A crossbowman of the contingent from the canton of Uri wears its black and yellow livery. He is the son of a prosperous craftsman, and his father has equipped him generously with a good quality German helmet and breastplate worn over a mail shirt. His bow is a modern type with a flat steel stave; although liable to become brittle and break in extremely cold weather it is immensely powerful.

(**Left**) He spans his bow with a *cranequin* - an efficient piece of engineering which is faster to operate than the older windlass and handy enough to be used on horseback. It works on the same principle as a modern car jack. The retaining loop is engaged over two pegs sticking out from the sides of the butt stock, and the hooks over the string. Winding the handle draws the string back by means of a ratchet bar, until it can be caught by the projection on the 'nut'.

(**Opposite top left**) His quiver is covered with water-repellent boarskin and has a tightly fitting lid, here tucked up under his belt, from which the cranequin hangs when not in use.

(**Opposite top right**) The short, heavy bolts or 'quarrells' have wood or parchment flights; this morning's issue from the supply wagons - where tens of thousands lie ready - have apparently been fletched with parchment cut from the pages of a looted book. A flat sprung clip holds the bolt in place ahead of the cord, which itself is held by the projecting step on top of the nut. Upward pressure on the trigger bar releases the nut to swivel forward, releasing the cord. (Photos John Howe)

Proofing Armour

As early as 1316 we have a record of mail being 'proved' against sword, axe, lance and bow. With the improved efficiency of missile weapons the strength of plate armour was usually tested with a shot from a crossbow or a gun at short range; some breastplates, and fewer helmets and backplates, bear the dent as 'proof' of quality. There were different degrees of proof - with a powerful crossbow and a sword, with a small lever crossbow and a javelin, and later with an arquebus and a pistol. A record of 1378 mentions tests using specially tempered *viretons*, crossbow bolts with spiral flights which set them revolving. Bolts for proofing armour could cost twice as much as normal. Once 'proved' the armour was officially stamped, and regulations existed to control its sale without such marks of quality.

(Right) The crossbowman's bearded officer, his helmet decorated with a turban, a plume, and the bull's head badge of Uri.

Beards were against the customs of the Latin church, and except for brief periods when fashion overcame custom they were rarely worn. Stubble might grow between the weekly shaves, as it does in peasant communities today. On campaign it might grow longer. Some might take an oath not to shave until some goal had been achieved, such as a pilgrimage. Charles the Bold grew a beard at one time and was copied by members of his court. Bearded men appear in biblical and historical paintings, but occasionally also in contemporary illustrations of soldiers. We read of one Burgundian sergeant who had his beard pulled in a tavern argument in Villiers-les-Hauts. (Photo Gerry Embleton)

Plunder

For a few lucky soldiers their service was both brief and startlingly profitable - and rarely more so than for some of the Swiss levies who marched against the Burgundians at Grandson and Morat in 1476.

When the Miller, Hans von Bruck and Jost Schindler from the little village of Ebikon stood shivering on the cold morning of 2 March on the snowy slopes above Concise, and saw the finest army in the world spread out below fresh from its merciless slaughter of the garrison of Grandson castle, they must have wondered if military service was, after all, a good idea.

A few hours later they were cavorting amid the ruins of an Aladdin's Cave of riches - the camp of the Duke of Burgundy's army and travelling court, fallen to them after hardly a battle, with the terrible invaders scattered in flight.

We know what plunder the three Ebikon men got. Or rather, we know what they told the clerks whose job it was to collect, evaluate and share out the loot. According to these official records their day had been somewhat disappointing. The Miller had half a leg armour (which he anyway claimed to have bought in Neuchâtel), one little banner, one big rope, one horse and a tablecloth. Hans von Bruck had one pair of hose (which he was wearing) and one gilded *paternoster* bead from a rosary, and wished - while the clerk was about it - to claim compensation for the loss of his pike in the heat of the fighting. Jost Schindler had a pair of knives …

We know from contemporary documents that all those hundreds of Swiss who handed in their modest loot with excuses ('I had a horse, but it ran away'; 'I got some armour, but someone stole it') were in fact busily squirrelling away cloth, gold, silver, arms, nails, sugar, tools, clothing, shoes and a thousand other things. In spite of searches, road blocks and arrests, many got away with it; and many a serious private fortune was made that day. (Photos: above Carlos Oliveira, right John Howe)

What did the three soldiers from Ebikon look like? We can try to guess. They were not poor men, but craftsmen earning craftsmen's wages. The earliest of the Schilling Chronicles and the Chronicle of Tschachtlan agree on the dress and equipment of the Swiss. They probably wore their own stout woollen doublet, hose and jacket; red and white seem to have been favourite military colours, but far from universal. Perhaps one or more had helmets: sallets, or small, deep bascinets, or round, narrow-brimmed kettle hats. The chronicles show many helmets of which we do not have surviving examples. Perhaps they wore twisted round them turbans in Ebikon's colours, or the blue and white of Lucerne canton.

They might have worn mail shirts with or without breastplates, or full plate upper body armour. The latter was the more likely if any or all of them carried the 17ft (5m) pike - once a Lucerne speciality, but by now skilfully used in massed formations all over what is now Switzerland. Otherwise they would probably have been armed with the halberd - a 6ft (1.8m) shaft with a long, shallow axehead drawn out into a broad spike at the end and a hook on the back. The weapons were supposed to be their own, but some might have been borrowed when the three were named as part of the conscripted 'Out-Troop' by the village council. They would have worn hoods and gowns against the weather, or carried them on their backs.

On the way home to Ebikon they were probably dirty, unshaven and tired - certainly exhilarated, but perhaps a little evasive, thinking of the bundles of plunder they had hidden in the woods for retrieval later. Unlike their neighbour Tscholij, who would stay on the battlefield forever, they were going home not just safe but richer men. (Photo Gerry Embleton)

15th Century Women on Campaign

Anna from Zurich - a travelling lady - was a follower of the Swiss army at Grandson. She got a share of the booty, probably more than she handed in. Beyond that we know nothing about her, nor, apart from a few names, anything about the thousands like her.

She pauses on the march, a noise up ahead - a rabbit for the pot? - or trouble? She has a light bow, and can use it. The Swiss chronicles occasionally show women armed with halberds, even one with a gun. We have occasional references to women, both nobles and commoners, taking up arms and fighting beside their men.

She wears all the clothes she owns - two shirts, a blue linen dress, a hood, and a old woollen coat 'found' among the wreckage of a pillaged hamlet. On her legs are woollen cloth hose, gartered below the knee, and stout boots. She is capable of, and equipped for, long hard marches and nights spent in the open. Under her hood she wears a typical headcloth over her plaited hair. In the centre is a small pewter *coquille St Jacques* badge, a relic of the pilgrimage to Compostella which she made some years before - in another life, it seems now …

She carries one of the big pewter canteens to serve the men around her; her blanket of cheap striped wool; and a well-stuffed haversack with some biscuit, cheese, smoked fish and dried apples. A small brass lantern, also 'found', hangs from her blanket roll. It will serve as a hearth in her bivouac tonight.

We may wonder if Anna took part in the Zurich contingent's forced march to relieve besieged Morat three months after the battle of Grandson - 87 miles (140km) in three days, and straight into battle. There, too, Charles the Bold's plans would come to nothing, leaving 12,000 Burgundian troops encircled and butchered on the field or driven into the lake to drown. (Photo Gerry Embleton)

Troops serving with well-organised commands were usually billeted on civilians, but in sparsely populated areas they made what shelters they could or slept in the open. Tents were not usually carried for the 'rank and file'. Stoutly made boots and shoes would have been necessary for all who marched, though it is surprising how often troops seem to have been mounted. There would have been a strong natural tendency to keep all one's belongings about one's person; other than those contingents owning wagons or packhorses, there was nowhere else to put spare clothes, cloaks, etc. Soldiers and their followers must have carried packs and bags, but we have almost no references to them.

Life for the women - and their children - must have been very hard, and downright cruel at times. Cold, hunger and fatigue would find out the weak and sickly and cut them down. There are mentions of severe frostbite during 15th century winter campaigns.

As for women's treatment by their fellow men, it certainly varied as widely as in the war zones of the 20th century. On the one hand, the still unchallenged Church of Rome 'set the moral agenda' throughout Europe; most people believed in God, the Devil, and a literal Heaven and Hell. Since before the Conquest the church had preached the moral duty of fighting men to spare and protect the weak - helpless peasants, women, children and the old.

On the other hand, it was believed that the stains a man put on his immortal soul even by 'mortal war' - total war against populations, marked by large-scale atrocities - could later be cleansed by repentance, confession, and donations. The fate of female camp followers after a defeat in enemy territory, or of villagers during the crushing of rebellion, must often have been hideous; but - just as in our own day - some would have found unexpected protectors. (Photos: above & above right Gerry Embleton; right David Lazenby, Middelaldercentret)

Armours

This is not a book about armour, a specific area of huge scope. Nevertheless, to simplify a complicated subject brutally, we may say here that the two main styles of plate armours in widespread use in the 15th century were the smoother, more rounded Italian, relying on large glancing surfaces; and the 'spikier' German style now called 'Gothic', characterised by an appearance of raised ridges and drawn-out points. The armourers of the two great centres of production - southern Germany, around Augsburg, Nuremberg and the Tyrol; and northern Italy, around Milan - copied each other, nevertheless. They exported their armours (and took their skills) all over Europe; and were widely copied in turn by the armourers of other countries - of which there were many, but about whom we know surprisingly little. Our ignorance may be due to the fact that libraries were destroyed and many sculptures and tomb effigies wantonly smashed by iconoclasts during the Reformation, various civil wars and the French Revolution. Some English effigies show armour of a very slightly different style (as do French, Burgundian and Spanish sculptures); but we cannot be sure if this is a purely native style, or represents armours imported from France or Flanders. Much research has still to be done, and it is only in recent years that definite English, Burgundian, French and Spanish styles have been given recognition.

(**Left & opposite**) These armours are worn by well-equipped soldiers of a garrison - horsemen who can extend the castle's circle of influence to a day's ride in any direction, or defend the castle itself, adapting the armour and weapons they possess to both tasks.

The armour is simple, typical of German export production. Each man's armour might as often be composed of separate purchases or captures as a completely matching harness. Much of the armour worn by soldiers - rather than nobles - must have been put together in this way. We read of the Pisa agent of an Avignon-based merchant instructed to buy up armour after the disbanding of a 'free company' in 1382 - 'for when peace is made they often sell all their armour'. (Photos Gerry Embleton)

There is a certain consistency in the rare surviving images and descriptions of what was worn under armour between c1460 and 1580. We see a logical development of practical foundation garments consisting of stoutly constructed doublet and hose, lightly padded where necessary, the seams strengthened with leather or webbing strips. Mail patches were sewn or laced on to cover vulnerable gaps between the plates, and points were attached to fix the plates on where necessary. The cut of these garments followed fashion; the 15th century armed man's silhouette was reflected in fashionable dress, and arming doublets seem to have been acceptable dress when out of armour. For evidence relating to these important garments see pages 82-83.

With help, a knight or man-at-arms' full armour was put on over this foundation in the following manner. A collar of mail was added first, buckled at the side or rear. Tight mail 'shorts' were tied on over the hose with points. The plate shoes (*sabetons*) were put on; then the *greaves* enclosing the calf, hinged vertically down the outside. The *cuisses* and *poleynes* (thigh and knee defences) came next, strapped against the legs and probably laced to the top of the hose. Breast and back plates followed, with the attached skirt piece or *fauld*, and were buckled down the right side. The arm and shoulder pieces were laced to the arming doublet and buckled about the arms in four parts: the *pauldron* protecting the shoulder, the *rarebrace* on the upper arm, the *couter* at the elbow, and the *vambrace* on the forearm. Spurs, helmet, sword and dagger completed the equipment.

(Opposite) Plate 9:
Garments worn under armour

(A) This illustration from the Bayeux Tapestry is clearly a much simplified symbolic rendering of a corpse being stripped, and should not be taken literally. Only a fool or a religious penitent would wear mail next to his naked skin.

(B) This more realistic image shows a garment worn under a mail shirt which is being pulled off over the head; the stance will be familiar to anyone who has worn the real thing. (English, Tickhill Psalter, c1303-1314)

(C) Separate-leg hose are laced with points to a solid-looking garment, probably a doublet cut very low and open between the thighs; some 15th century fencing illustrations show similar arrangements. (French, Livre des Nobles Femmes, late 14th C)

(D) Mail shirt worn over a stiffened and dagged coat. (Song of Roland, 14th C)

(E) One important later 15th century illustrated text is headed 'How a man schall be armyd at his ese when he schal fighte on foote'. In modern spelling it reads, in part: 'He shall have no shirt upon him, but a doublet of fustian lined with satin, cut full of holes. The doublet must be strongly bound where the points are set about the great (part) of the arm, and the gussets of mail must be sewed to the doublet at the bend of the arm. The arming points must be made of fine twine such as men used to make strings for crossbows, and ... tied small and pointed as points. They must be waxed with shoe-maker's wax ... He shall have a pair of hose of worsted cloth, and a pair of short pads of thin blanket to put about his knees to prevent chafing ...; also a pair of shoes of thick leather ... fastened with small whipcord ... and three cords must be fast sewed to the heel of the shoe, and fine cords in the middle of the sole ...'.

In 1434 John Hill, armourer to Henry VI of England, mentions 'hose of cord without vamps ... cut at the knees and lined with linen cloth on the bias'; and 'shoes of red leather thin laced and fretted underneath with whipcord ...'.

(F, J & K) Rare illustrations of garments worn under armour in the 16th century 'Illustrated Inventory' of the Royal Armoury, Madrid, look remarkably like their earlier counterparts.

(G) Juan de la Abadia's painting of St Michael may show the 'hose of cord' referred to under E. (Spanish, last quarter 15th C)

(H) Portrait of an Italian gentleman (by Moroni, c1550), showing exactly the same sort of components as earlier arming doublets, with leather- or fabric-edged mail panels tied on with metal-tipped points. Only the fashionable mid-16th century cut betrays the date.

(I) *Braies d'acier* often appear in 15th century manuscripts; and at least one document orders them to be worn - the Burgundian Ordinance of St Maximin de Trèves, October 1473.

(L) The King of France's Scottish archer guard were painted by Jean Fouquet in 1458 wearing their grey arming doublets reinforced witèh black leather or webbing strips.

(M) The same construction appears in a Burgundian tapestry (The Siege of Jerusalem, c1460) and several other sources.

(N) Hypothetical reconstruction of mid-15th century arming doublet; red and grey seem to have been favourite colours. It is made of several layers of sturdy linen but not excessively padded, cut to facilitate movement, tight-fitting to avoid uncomfortable wrinkles, and with all seams and edges reinforced with leather or webbing. It might be covered with fustian or some richer material. Contact with armour would soon wear into it a pattern of dirty oil stains, and sweat would stain it with salt 'tide marks'.

(O) A late 15th century German painting shows details of a reinforced doublet lined with black cloth, slipped back off the shoulders with the hanging sleeves turned inside out.

(P) This early 16th century arming jacket (visible in a painting by Giorgione, c1515) follows contemporary fashion but earlier details of construction. Note the two rivets and washers to further strengthen the reinforcing strips.

(Q & R) Padded helmet caps were worn to supplement the helmet lining. In the 1460s a padded and often decorated roll was worn encircling the head. There is no truth in the illogical suggestion that the 'bowl crop' hairstyle of the first half of the century was useful for 'padding' the head. At the end of the century the then fashionably long hair was caught up in a netted cap which fitted neatly inside a sallet, a fashion drawn by Dürer and Cranach among other early 16th century artists.

(S) Several surviving adjustable 16th century arming caps in the Kunsthistorisches Museum, Vienna, offer tantalising clues to the probably sophisticated construction of earlier examples.

(Left The 15th century description quoted under (E) mentions a fustian doublet lined with 'satene cutt full of hoolis' (holes) - i.e., worked all over with round holes bound with strong twine, like the eyelet holes in doublet and hose to take the points. This gives an extremely strong but well-ventilated foundation garment. There are occasional mentions of this technique in contemporary documents, and some surviving examples; one mid-15th century German example has a brass ring sewn into each hole. (Photo Gerry Embleton)

A

B

C

D

E

F

G

H

I

J

K

L

M

N

O

P

Q

R

S

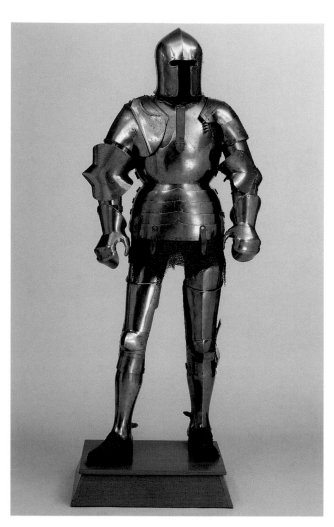

(**Left**) We have space to present here just one superb medieval example of the armourer's art, made in Milan c1450 and now in the Burrell Collection. Armour was beaten out, hammered and hardened. Water-powered hammers were widely used for the very rough work. Then the plates were beaten and expertly shaped by hand - thinned where one plate passed over another, left thick where blows might fall. Generations of apprentices strove to become masters in an immensely demanding profession. Today's smiths simply cannot compete.

This was the sort of armour worn by knight and captain, the 'top of the market'. Armour was available in different qualities right down to surprisingly cheap, second-hand, and refurbished. But it was never crudely formed; men's lives depended upon the exact interplay of the different plates. It was produced by a well-established industry for a professional and demanding international clientele. (Photo Glasgow Museums / The Burrell Collection)

(**Below**) Three different examples of riveted mail, probably 15th - 16th centuries, one piece (bottom right) edged with brass rings. Mail was made in many different grades, sizes and weights and is almost impossible to date accurately. Since it is made from iron wire it is very vulnerable to rusting; it is hardly surprising that most surviving medieval examples are fragmentary and of uncertain provenance. However, if carefully cleaned and oiled - as at least some mail must have been, throughout the ages when it was a valuable commodity - it lasts almost indefinitely. Not all of the mail used by the common soldiers was brand new and in good repair; in fact, it is perfectly plausible to suppose that some very ancient mail may still have been in use at the end of the Middle Ages. (Photo Gerry Embleton)

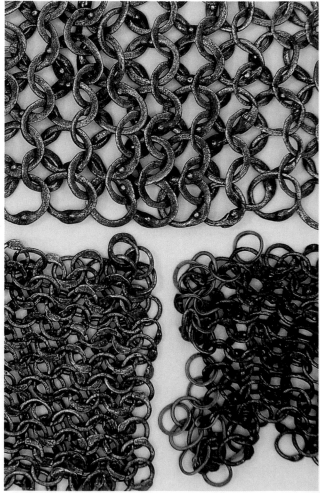

Where has all the armour gone? Medieval armour is rare today; not one clearly identifiable English-made armour survives from before the reign of Henry VIII (1509-1547). Most of what does survive is the armour of kings and lords, kept for its historical or aesthetic value. What happened to all the rest? Armours were, after all, produced on an industrial scale for many generations, and tens of thousands of 'harnesses' must have been exported all over the Continent from the great factories of Germany and Italy, even if we discount production for the home market in other countries.

It has been lost in war and shipwreck. Obsolete, it has rusted away in forgotten stacks in arsenals or attics. Deemed useless, it has been used to corduroy paths, make cooking pots and door fittings, or chopped into small plates for brigandines and jacks.

In 1575 Sir George Howard, Master of the Armouries in the Tower of London, was ordered to convert old armours into 1,500 jacks for sea service. In 1635 Charles I retained armour for 10,000 men at the Tower, but ordered the rest sold to people who had none: we can only guess at what pieces, which would today be regarded as treasures, ended up on the heads of militiamen. Collections began early - in the Royal Armouries, in arsenals, and later, when armour was going out of fashion, as curiosities. With a few notable exceptions, most of the great stocks of 'ammunition' armour simply went into the melting pot. What we have left is a very uneven collection, with many fine 15th century German and Italian armours but no recognisable English examples.

Of the hundreds of thousands of helmets made during the 'Middle Ages' only a handful have come down to us. From these we tend to draw sweeping conclusions, attempting to chart a system of types and their development. Illustrations show many helmets in common use of which no example survives. The commonest types were a range of shallow visorless sallets, from skullcaps with almost no neck guard to those with a deep neck guard **(above left)**. Sallets with visors **(above)**, or made without a movable visor but deep-fronted with eyeslits **(left)**, were popular in the 15th century. Most helmets were polished bright, but some were left black from the forge, blued, browned or - **(left)** - painted with designs and mottoes. Kettle hats and bowl-shaped helmets, ranging from something like US and British World War II shapes to splendid deep-brimmed affairs with twisted, fluted crowns, were also very popular.
(Photos: above John Howe, left Gerry Embleton)

Landsknechts

This Landsknecht hand-gunner of c1515 is still wearing his finery at the start of a campaign, and shows many of the characteristic details outlined on Plates 10 and 11 (pages 89-91). Over a white coif he wears an extravagantly plumed hat tied firmly beneath his chin. Unusually, his doublet buttons down the front; more common was a plastron front fastened by hooks and eyes or points at the left of the chest. His tight hose are made of fine woollen cloth and reach far enough up the waist to be self-supporting. Between them and his doublet his ample shirt bulges out. Around his neck hangs a brass powder flask; and his typical short sword is tied around his waist in a nearly horizontal position.

His main armament is a heavily stocked brass-barrelled matchlock, little more sophisticated than those introduced in the 1470s. Modern tests show these to be no slower to reload, nor dramatically less accurate - against a massed target - than flintlock muskets. (Photos John Howe)

(Opposite) Plate 10:
Swiss and German Infantry, c1500-1525

The origins of the slashed clothing so popular among Swiss and German (*Landsknecht*) mercenaries at the beginning of the 16th century are obscure. The usual folktale is that Swiss soldiers slashed tight-fitting clothing captured during their victories over the Burgundians in 1476, so that they could wear it with less strain. This is clearly implausible. Clothing had been looted for generations; most 15th century hose and many doublets were tight-fitting, but went unslashed. There is no evidence that Swiss and Germans were physically any bigger than those they killed and looted (and in fact, they often killed and looted each other). Far from all being the massively-built 'mountaineers' of romantic legend which some modern historians love to perpetuate, many 'Swiss' troops of the day were craftsmen, townsfolk and valley villagers. The many surviving illustrations clearly show properly constructed 'purpose-made' slashed garments; there is no sign that they are civilian clothes cut about by the wearer.

(A, B & C) These show the development of the panoply of ostrich plumes attached to caps and turbans by the Swiss - particularly officers and banner-bearers - across the turn of the 15th/16th centuries. Although worn by some Landsknechts they do seem to have been characteristically Swiss adornments.

We should remember, however, that there was no clear national or geographic separation between the communities of what are now northern Switzerland and southern Germany, resulting in a certain flexibility of loyalties and fashions, and most troops of the Swiss Confederation thought of themselves as 'Germans'. The Imperial troops parading in the woodcut series *Maximilian's Triumph* (c1515) include three named Swiss - Peter von Winterthur, Fleck and Hein Oterle. Indeed, mercenaries of many nationalities served in these bands; the *'Triumph'* also names

'Richard Vantos, Englishman' and 'Juan Talsat, Spaniard' as 'meritorious soldiers'.

(D) A striking feature of late 15th/ early 16th century costume was the development of the 'codpiece' (nicknamed *pont-levis* or 'drawbridge' in French), from a simple, practical flap in the groin of the hose to a heavily padded and later slashed and beribboned advertisement for the wearer's claimed masculinity. It inspired many a bawdy tale. One reads of a gentleman who kept his purse, handkerchief, and even oranges in his codpiece; and of Hans von Schweinichen, who sewed 50 gold pieces into his, but sadly had them stolen while in Cologne …

(E, F & G) During the first decade of the 16th century hose were divided into two parts: 'upper stocks', i.e. breeches, and stockings. These were often sewn together again as one garment - see G; or they could be fastened with points and worn with one or both stockings turned down - see F. (H) Points - woven or leather

ribbons tipped with a metal tag - were laced through two matching pairs of holes and tied with a single bow, in the same manner that hose were fastened to the doublet. The bows might be left on display or carefully tucked out of sight.

(I) Reconstruction of a typical Swiss costume of c1520. The low-necked jacket had to be securely fastened across the chest - in this case by hooks-and-eyes and points - to take the strain of the heavy padded sleeves and tight waist. Experience with physical reconstructions shows that if the jacket is unfastened the weight of the sleeves tends to drag it back off the shoulders - a feature clearly seen in contemporary illustrations.

(J) Back view of another example, this one high-necked. The doublet and high-waisted hose were often worn unfastened from one another, the points hanging free and the shirt blousing out between them. The voluminous slashing and padding would have given some

protection against cutting blows in battle.

(K) Composite drawing of various details taken from prints and drawings of soldiers on campaign. It was fashionable to wear one leg, or part of it, naked - which was of course cooler in the hot Swiss and Italian summers. Mercenaries seem often to have been ragged, stripped of plumes, bare-legged and wearing broken shoes or sandals - but always ready to cover themselves in finery come payday and a parade.

(L & M) Leather 'overalls' were more popular among Landsknechts than Swiss, but were worn by both. They seem to have been made from fairly flexible leather, though occasionally very thick, and would have made a light and pretty effective protection.

(N) The chain armour 'splints' worn in the late 15th century seem to have been still in use in the early 16th, in this case worn with breastplate and fauld.

(Left) This grim Swiss captain wears fashionable slashed clothes, but the feathers are gone. He wears a simple skullcap helmet, and is wrapped in his cloak against a chill summer rain. He is on his way down to Italy and must cross the high pass; pray God for good weather and a quick campaign …
(Photo Anne Embleton)

A 1500

1501
B

C 1508

°1500
D

E 1502

F

G 1512

°1520
I

1515

H

J

K 1512

L 1510

M

1515

N

89

Landsknecht banner-bearer and his woman, c1515. (Photo John Howe)

(Opposite) Plate 11: Reislaufer and Landsknecht, c1515-1525

Neatly tailored slashings to ease the movement of shoulder and elbow appear in Italian costume, and then in Swiss and German, during the latter part of the 15th century; among civilians and mercenaries towards 1500; and bursting into a great flourish in 1500-1520. It is interesting that the 1513 Lucerne Chronicle shows many Swiss soldiers but few slashed garments, while the works of Swiss artists Urs Graf and Niklaus Manuel (who both served as soldiers in the Italian wars) show a lot. *Maximilian's Triumph* - a series of woodcuts of c1515 depicting a great triumphal military parade - shows much slashing. By 1520-1530 the style had spread to the courts of Europe, although with many national and regional differences.

Although all of the wide variety of styles were shared by Swiss and Germans, there seem to have been certain details, or combinations of details, which each side associated mostly with the other. Individually it may have been difficult to tell friend from foe, but *en masse* a collective 'look' made them recognisable. Here is a glimpse of how Swiss artists caricatured themselves, the *Reislaufer*; their allies the French; and their enemies, the *Landsknechts*.

(A) Caricature of a typical Landsknecht by the Swiss soldier/artist Urs Graf.

(B, C & D) A wonderful view of foe, friend and employer seen through the experienced eye of Urs Graf:

(B) A Landsknecht. This representation is perhaps equivalent to a modern cartoon 'American' identified by a Stetson and cowboy boots - instantly recognisable, but hardly a realistic interpretation of the average US citizen.

(C) A Swiss Reislaufer.

(D) A French recruiting officer. He is a more conservatively dressed figure; the heavily slashed 'German' style was less popular in France. Interestingly he displays on his arm a fleurde-lys badge, perhaps in yellow, which is also depicted on a Swiss in another of Graf's drawings - see (E). We do not know how widely this and other identifying badges were worn, apart from the frequently depicted white Swiss cross and the St Andrew's saltire of the Empire.

(F) Rear view of a Landsknecht showing the construction of the hat and how it was worn slung on the back. His sword is the typical short, double-edged German infantry 'Katzbalger' or 'Cat-Mangler'. His hobnailed spare shoes are tied to his halberd, a detail drawn by Urs Graf.

(G) A typical Swiss on campaign, his purse around his neck and his gaudy clothes beginning to show signs of wear and tear. Both Urs Graf and Niklaus Manuel frequently show soldiers reduced to rags and tatters. Sandals might replace worn-out shoes during the Italian wars. The long hand-and-a-half sword is more Swiss than Landsknecht, but there is really nothing about this figure that could not equally have been worn by a German. The constant fighting, looting, and consequent interchange of clothing and weapons must have made them indistinguishable at times.

(H) This cap, with its brim slit to make two pointed 'ears', is shown by Urs Graf and may have been a transitory Swiss fashion.

(I) This wonderful print by Urs Graf compares a German Landsknecht (left) with a Swiss Reislaufer (right), exaggerating the former's flat cap, moustache, and S-shaped sword quillons.

(J) For comparison we show here the costume worn by a typical German peasant at the end of the 15th century - old fashioned, and showing none of the exaggerations of his oppressors' dress styles. Wagoners and followers accompanying the mercenary armies frequently wore clothing like this.

Early 16th Century Armour

Although the soldier's more gaudily noticeable dress may draw our eye away from armour, at least partial harness was still in widespread use by footsoldiers and horsemen alike. The extent to which the increased use of firearms negated its value should not be over-emphasised. Although the greater weight and expense of bullet-proof armour probably limited its use mostly to cavalry, and although matchlock balls could certainly punch through most 'ammunition' breastplates, the major threat to the footsoldier would still come from blade weapons for several generations to come. We may suppose that at least half the infantry of this period carried pikes and other blade weapons, and fought most often against men similarly armed; these massed clashes of great human 'hedgehogs' tipped with steel demanded at least upper body armour.

The armour of the wealthy continued the medieval tradition of decoration and display. Many great princes and their courtiers and guards wore richly decorated armours. Engraving (the cutting of fine lines into the surface) and etching (the cutting of designs into the metal with acid) reached a high point in the 16th century. When the lines were filled with blacking, and the polished plates gilded or silvered, a magnificent effect was produced. Armour embossed with high-relief decoration also appeared at the end of the 15th century, reaching dizzy heights of fantasy in the 'parade' armours of the 16th.

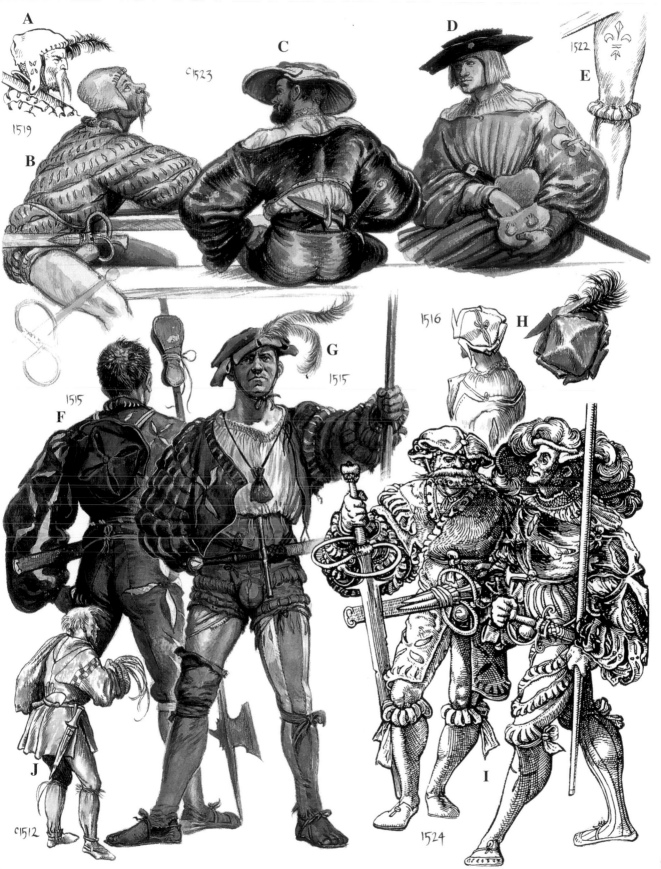

A
1519
B
C
c1523
D
1522
E
1516
H
G
1515
F
1515
J
c1512
I
1524

91

Shown here are three styles of shoes worn by the early 16th century Landsknechts and Swiss. Your reconstructed historical shoes should be robust, stand up to long marches, not let in water, and be comfortable. If not, there is something wrong with your experiment. (Photos: top and bottom, John Howe; centre, Gerry Embleton)

(**Left**) Practical and comfortable broad-toed ankle boots which fasten with a long strap, very like the peasant boots of the period.

(**Right**) Wide-toed '*Kuhmäule*' - 'cow's mouth' shoes. Experiments show these to be comfortable as long as they fit well around heel and instep.

(**Left**) The shoes most often depicted in drawings and prints are shallow, wide-toed, and cut so that the front of the shoe barely covers the toes. In spite of being tied on to the foot they are comfortable enough for a sedate walk; but to run over broken ground and to fight in them is almost impossible. Perhaps the more extravagant styles were kept for parades and 'walking out'? These shoes were made to be worn and tested by David McCabe of 'Time Farer' - a master craftsman with a rare eye for the shape and 'feel' of historical shoes.

(**Left**) This shows how the doublet can now be left securely fastened to the hose by points and slipped off the shoulders - something of a relief when one becomes overheated by the voluminous slashings and paddings of the doublet.

(**Below left & below**) Steel skullcaps or small sallets were often worn, as was body armour. For most this was usually limited to a breastplate or breast-and-back; but sometimes - like this officer in an elegant long-tailed sallet - they wore beautifully fluted and decorated German field armour. This example is perhaps a little old-fashioned for 1515, but for all but the very rich armour that still functioned and fitted was too valuable to be discarded for mere fashion. (Photos John Howe)

Tailpiece: Recreating Medieval Costume

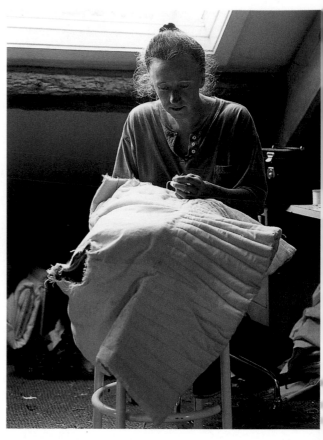

Re-enactment is *the* hobby for many thousands of people. It gives pleasure to participants and public alike, and - at its best - it can open the public's mind and heart to their past. First and foremost it should be enjoyable. If done in front of a paying public, it should entertain. If it claims to 'educate' then it should try to tell the truth. If it claims 'accuracy' then it should be judged on how well it lives up to that claim - and it is not easy.

No one can (or would want to) accurately re-enact a battle; that has to be a piece of theatre which paints the scene with a very broad brush. But scenes from everyday life - craftsmen at work, military training, camp life, sports - can all be extremely interesting if recreated carefully.

To recreate any small slice of the past, and certainly medieval military costume, takes a steadily increasing amount of work the more closely we look at it. We can never know what it was really like, never be 100 % accurate; but we can try as hard as we can to strip away the misconceptions, the Hollywood myths - indeed, the myths that our history books perpetuate. If you are going to give an impression of the past that 'works' when viewed from ten yards away, then you can get away with all sorts of shortcuts and compromises; nevertheless, you will still have to try to get the shapes of arms and armour and the cut of clothing right, like any good filmmaker. But if you go for 'hands-on' reconstructions, to be viewed from ten inches rather than ten yards, then you really do have a lot of work ahead of you.

You cannot claim that 'this is an accurate reconstruction of exactly what it was like' if you use nylon cloth which doesn't behave or hang like wool, or 'armour' which has demanded no greater metalworking skills than available at your local panel-beater. Real armour fits and works perfectly, it doesn't clank and rattle and jam. Handmade tools were better than modern mass-produced ones; skilled hand-sewing is finer than modern machine-sewing.

Everything you recreate will have to be convincing, and therefore thoroughly researched from contemporary references. You will have to try to become a passable - if not a master-craftsman. You will have to accept that many things are simply

(Above) Angela Essenhigh of 'Seams Historic', the creator of many of the costumes in this book, at work on a real jack - the air filled with muffled curses, cries of pain and the snap of breaking needles …
(Photo Anne Embleton)

(Left) The pleasures of re-enactment: a 'family' gathering of members of the Company of St George in the castle of Lenzburg in Switzerland, with nothing modern in sight.
(Photo Gerry Embleton)

94

(**Left**) Paul Denny of 'Artefacts' and a young apprentice shoot walnuts across the castle keep of Haute Koenigsbourg in Alsace - hoping, no doubt, to attract purchasers of slightly larger versions …
(Photo Gerry Embleton)

(**Below**) A remarkable example of experimental archaeology. In 1998 David Lazenby and his team at the Middelaldercentret in Denmark reconstructed a 15th century leather diving suit, metal helmet, lead-weighted pattens and a bellows-fed air supply. The suit was based on contemporary documentation and was, with care, practical to a depth of 5.5m (18 feet). The experiment does not prove that such suits ever got beyond the pages of the inventors' notebooks; but it does show that they were possible, within the realms of known technology and available materials. (Photo Andreas Jensen, Middelaldercentret)

beyond our capabilities today; the skills are lost to us. We don't have the money to create a truly convincing knight, his tent, horses and equipment - let alone a duke. Recreating a washerwoman or a common archer is hard enough - how many of us can draw and shoot a 100lb-plus bow?

If you are trying to look like a real medieval soldier or camp follower, remember that they were not wearing funny 'costumes' but strongly made clothes for work and outdoor life. Choose the best woollens and linen you can afford; get the cut right; move in your clothes - imagine that you will have to live in them night and day, in the open, rain or shine. You will have to spend half of that time marching over rough roads, carrying all you need on your back. If you are recreating a soldier then you may have to run, jump, tumble and fight, to cross streams and push your way through woods and brambles.

Do you still think your costume and kit are realistic? Do they at least look as if they could stand up to the test? The more practical you can make your clothes, the better they will feel on you and the more convincing you will look.

It is better to be patient and get a few pieces of good, simple kit for a humble soldier or follower than to rush to portray a knight in armour which looks like tin - or a noble lady in gaudy man-made fibres, which will look nothing like fine period fabrics (and will go up like a torch if you get too close to the campfire).

We hope the illustrations in this book will encourage and help you. Making them has been a valuable experience and something of an experiment. Whether or not you get your pleasure from trying to be accurate, always remember that there are a lot of different ways to help history come alive and something is to be learned from all of them. Keep an open mind, share what you learn, and never be afraid to admit - and correct - the mistakes you make. Help and encourage others; and above all, have fun.

GAE
Prêles
May 2000

(David Lazenby , Middelaldercentret)

Acknowledgments

Sadly there is not enough space here to thank by name everyone whose kindness and generosity has made this book possible. I must say a special 'thank you' to all my friends in the Company of St George and their guests, for sharing their knowledge and experience over the years, and for posing in all weathers. Thanks also to the members of Wolfbane, the White Company, the Black Prince's Household, the Lincoln Castle Bowmen, to Dominic Delgrange of the Compagnie Lys et Lion, and to Eli Tanner; to the directors and staff of the many castles and museums which opened their doors to us; to costumiers Angela Essenhigh, Julie Douglass and Marina Harrington; to craftsmen Simon Metcalfe, Will Hutt, Paul Denny, Matt Champion, Ian Ashdown and John Buttifint; to photographers David Lazenby, Anne Embleton, Philippe Krauer of *L'Illustré*, Ian Ashdown, Carlos Oliveira, Simon Metcalfe, Alan and Michael Perry and Andreas Jensen. In particular I would like to thank John Howe for his considerable help, teamwork and constant support. Thanks to the models for many patient hours clambering about the rocks and woods; to Martin Windrow, who has been far more than an editor of this book, for his help and encouragement and for turning my stockfish stew into bouillabaisse; and last but not least to my wife Anne, for her enthusiastic translations of medieval French and German, her hours of typing, and for Sam and Camille, who helped take some of the pictures ...

Further Reading

There are no books available that treat our subject in detail. We have consulted far more individual sources that we can list here; instead we recommend the following to supplement subjects we have only touched upon:

Fashion and costume:
A.Harmand, *Jeanne d'Arc*, Librairie Ernest Leroux (Paris,1929)
M.Houston, *Medieval Costume in England and France*, Adam & Charles Black (1979)
M.Hald, *Ancient Danish Textiles from Bogs and Burials*, National Museum of Denmark (1980)
G.R.Owen-Crocker, *Dress in Anglo-Saxon England*, Manchester University Press (1986)
S.M.Newton, *Fashion in the Age of the Black Prince*, Boydell Press (1980)

Daily and military life:
P.Aries & G.Duby, *A History of Private Life*, The Belknap Press (1988)
P.Contamine, *La Guerre au Moyen Age*, Presses Universitaires de France (1980)

Arms and armour:
D. Edge & J.Paddock, *Arms and Armour of the Medieval Knight*, Defoe Publishing (1988)
N.Michael, *Armies of Medieval Burgundy 1364-1477*, Osprey Publishing (1983)
A.V.B.Norman & D.Pottinger, *Warrior to Soldier 449-1660*, Wiedenfeld & Nicolson Ltd (1966)

Soldiers:
G.A.Embleton & J.Howe, *The Medieval Soldier*, Windrow & Greene (1994)
M.Prestwich, *Armies and Warfare of the Middle Ages*, Yale University Press (1996)
J.R.Hale, *Artists and Warfare in the Renaissance*, Yale University Press (1990)

Middelaldercentret

The Middle Ages Centre is an open-air 'living history' museum near Nykobing Falster in Denmark. Aside from being an award-winning tourist attraction, the Centre is involved with on-going research and reconstruction of subjects relating to Denmark in the Middle Ages, and in particular to the late 14th century. A great deal of emphasis is placed on historical accuracy and attention to detail. The museum houses a medieval harbour, several reconstructions of Danish archaeological ship and boat finds, and numerous buildings and workshops. A number of crafts are practised using copies of 14th century tools and implements, and can be seen on a daily basis.

The photographs of Middelaldercentret scenarios used in this book were taken by the museum's Design and Development Director, David Lazenby. David is also a well-known wildlife, adventure and underwater photographer whose images of wild and remote places are regularly featured in international publications.